Midge in Lebanon

By
Mildred Thompson Olson

TEACH Services, Inc.
PUBLISHING
www.TEACHServices.com • (800) 367-1844

World rights reserved. This book or any portion thereof may not be copied or reproduced in any form or manner whatever, except as provided by law, without the written permission of the publisher, except by a reviewer who may quote brief passages in a review.

The author assumes full responsibility for the accuracy of all facts and quotations as cited in this book. The opinions expressed in this book are the author's personal views and interpretations, and do not necessarily reflect those of the publisher.

This book is provided with the understanding that the publisher is not engaged in giving spiritual, legal, medical, or other professional advice. If authoritative advice is needed, the reader should seek the counsel of a competent professional.

Copyright © 2019 TEACH Services, Inc.
ISBN-13: 978-1-57258-341-2 (Paperback)
Library of Congress Control Number: 2005926898

Published by

www.TEACHServices.com • (800) 367-1844

DEDICATION

I want to dedicate this book to my children Ronnalee (Netteburg) and David who endured many hardships with us in North Lebanon. I also want to include our younger children, Bekki (Gardner) and Ronda (Portsche). For no reason other than love, I mention the seven grandchildren who are our pride and joy—Charity, Kristin, and Olen Netteburg, Hans and Heidi Olson, and Jonathan and Lindsay Gardner.

APPRECIATION

We appreciated all of our fellow missionaries who became our overseas family. Among those who gave us special encouragement during our first term of mission service were: George and Mary Keough, Arthur and Dora Keough, Bob and Jeannette Mole, Edith Davis, Shahin Ilter, Jim and Carolyn Russell, Ruby Williams, and George and Laura Appel.

Special appreciation goes to Moses Ghazal and Michael Kebbas who worked untiringly with us over a period of four years. Through bombs, stones, dynamite, threats, and sickness they were courageous. They never deserted their posts of duty or us when things became impossible. Through the trials we endured together we developed a special bond of friendship, love, and respect. No one else can take the special place of Moses and Michael in our hearts.

Lastly I appreciate the help of my husband, Wayne Olson, and friend, Esther Tarangle, for editing my manuscript, and son-in-law, Kermit Netteburg, for editing and transferring the story into book form.

PREFACE

We might have fainted with fear had we known the awesome experiences that lay in the perilous path ahead of us when we accepted the call to pioneer the Adventist message in North Lebanon. We would be plagued by government red tape, religious persecution, and serious illnesses. We would be bombed, dynamited, stoned, and ambushed.

We were innocent, ambitious kids in our early twenties thoroughly dedicated to our assignment. We had no experience in devising ways to present the gospel of Jesus love in areas where no Seventh-day Adventist members existed, but God had a strategy unknown or imagined by us. He would reveal it to us bit by bit as it was needed. First, He arranged a providential meeting with Edmond Shammas from North Lebanon. Next, Edmond introduced us to his friends in Tripoli and his family in Shekka with whom we began studying the Bible. Then, severe religious persecution developed along the seacoast region, and we moved on into the mountains where the gospel flourished and never died out. Eventually we preached in more than a dozen towns and villages, but it was never easy. Constant attempts on our lives kept us alert and dependent on God. Through one miracle after another, He preserved us.

With the help of national ministers—Michael Kebbas, Moses Ghazal, Farris Bishi, Maurice Katrib, Noel Abdul Messiah, and Joseph Fargo—the work expanded rapidly. Leading Lebanese families that assisted and encouraged us were the Haddads, Shamases, Melkies,

MIDGE IN LEBANON

Akars, Jabbours, Muellims, Jehas, Razzouks, Simaans, Deebs, Solimans, Nabtis, and others.

The people who went through these experiences with us have read the manuscript and have ascertained that, to the best of their memory, it happened as I have told it. I was able to pin-point exact dates and numbers from my husband's record/diary books that he has kept for 40 years. Then I drew details from the Middle East folder where I had recorded outstanding events as they transpired lest, through the years, my memory of them might grow dim. In most cases, I have used the correct names of people and places. In some instances, however, I have used pseudonyms to protect the privacy of the persons involved in the events depicted.

This is the history of the beginning of the Adventist work in North Lebanon and of the people who responded to God's message of peace and salvation. But it is more. Hopefully, the rehearsal of these experiences will increase the reader's confidence in God who loves us so very much, and, when necessary, still performs miracles for us today.

Almost forty years have passed into eternity since the events related in these pages transpired, but time can never efface the experiences which made this book possible. The stone-dented pulpit standing in the Bishmizeen church today is a grim reminder of the persecution we endured. Converts from North Lebanon are still courageously carrying the message of God to the world.

Because we are apt to forget that God still controls this wild world, the following passage convinced me that I should record our experiences:

As those who have spent their lives in the service of Christ draw near to the close of their earthly ministry, they will be impressed by the Holy Spirit to recount the

PREFACE

experiences they have had in connection with the work of God. The record of His wonderful dealings with His people, of His Goodness in delivering them from trial, should be repeated to those newly come to the faith. (White, Acts of the Apostles, p. 574.)

Contents

1	Guess What, Mom?	1
2	Arabic!?!.	5
3	Ship Ahoy, and All that Stuff	13
4	Excitement in Beirut	23
5	The Long Dreadful Night	31
6	Hi Ho, hi Ho, It's Off to Work We Go	37
7	Falling in Love	45
8	To Move or Not to Move, That Was the Question	51
9	To the Shores of Tripoli.	63
10	Starts and Stops	69
11	A Well is a Hole in the Ground	75
12	Trouble in the Wheat Field	83
13	Students Without a School	95
14	"Please, God, Spare the Child"	99
15	Shekka is No Mecca.	107
16	Through the Dark Valley	119
17	Go Tell It on the Mountain.	131
18	"Blast 'Em Out".	141
19	Give Us this Day our Daily Bread—And Time to Eat It	145
20	The Step to Success	157
21	The Explosion???!!	161
22	The Battle for Bishmizeen.	177
23	After the Battle	197
24	Potpourri	203
25	The Humorous and Not so Humorous.	211
26	Shaking Dust	223

MIDGE IN LEBANON

27 Coping with Death 243
28 The Least of His Little Ones 249
29 Countdown Time 253
30 Final Days. 261
    Appendix 265

The young missionary family: David, Midge, Wayne, and Ronnalee.

CHAPTER 1

GUESS WHAT, MOM!

Wayne and I were ecstatic! We had just received and read the most exciting news in print. We rushed from our shack on the outskirts of Fort Scott, Kansas, into the middle of town where we could find a pay phone. My hands shook as I jabbed at the operator button and put in my request for a collect call to Colman, South Dakota.

Mom answered the phone. "Mildred? Is something wrong?"

"No, Mom, everything is absolutely perfect—almost divine. Guess what? We just received a letter today, July 14, 1945, from Elder Bradley of the General Conference inviting us to study German at the seminary in preparation to going to Europe as missionaries. Who knows, maybe I'll end up in your old stomping ground, Bredstedt, Germany. What do you think of that?"

"I, ah, I, ah, don't know what to think just yet. I'm sort of stunned."

"Why, Mom? Are you stunned because I'm going to be a missionary? I always promised God I would be if He saw fit to call me to that sacred work."

"No, I always believed you would be a missionary. I'm just surprised that a call for mission service came to you only two months after Wayne finished college. I am also astonished that they would call you as missionaries to Europe. I could understand you being called to Asia, Africa, or South America—like your sister Lela, Ray, and baby Jerry going to Brazil—but Europe? I'd think they already had enough ministers over there."

"Well, I guess they don't. Here is what Elder Bradley says in his letter: 'The General Conference has recognized that when Europe opened up again, we would be called upon not only to help with money and equipment, but also with a large number of specially trained workers for the rehabilitation of our work on that continent...(The) committee has today taken action inviting you to accept appointment as missionaries to Europe, and to study the German language in preparation for service in due time somewhere on that continent.' There's a lot more too. But in essence he says that we should first pass physical examinations, then be in Washington, D.C., by September 9 when classes begin."

"Well, it all sounds wonderful, and I'm thrilled that my prayers for you have been answered," Mom said with a slight tremor in her voice. "God bless."

"Thanks, Mom, we believe He will. We love you. Goodbye."

Next we shared our good news with Wayne's parents. Then we called the doctor to get appointments for our physicals. We completed them in two days and mailed the doctor's recommendation to Elder Bradley. "Fit as two frisky calves." (The doc was a country boy.)

The next week we received the committee's approval and our health clearance. We mailed back our autobiographical information and pictures. Now we were all set except for one matter of unfinished business—the evangelistic effort in Fort Scott.

By the end of August the effort was finished, and we had fulfilled our obligations to the Kansas Conference. We said goodbye to Elder McWilliams and family, the Piersons, Eppels, and the other wonderful church

GUESS WHAT, MOM!

people, loaded up our little trailer, and headed for Washington, D.C. After five days of travel, we drove into Takoma Park, found the General Conference building, and informed Elder Bradley that we were the Olsons reporting for duty.

What a disappointment awaited us!

CHAPTER 2

ARABIC ! ?

Elder Bradley's face was wreathed in smiles as we exchanged introductions. "I've got a surprise for you," he said, his face still glowing. "The mission board has canceled the German class, so we're asking you six couples scheduled to study German to take the Arabic class instead. We believe that the Arab lands are much more in need of missionaries right now."

I almost swooned out of my chair. "A—ARAB LANDS?" I exploded, rocking with shock at the news.

"Yes. You know—Egypt, Jordan, Palestine, Lebanon, Syria, Iraq, Libya," he answered, oblivious to my reaction. "The seminary's first Arabic class members are already in the field—Neal and Eleanor Wilson, Edith Davis, Ruby Williams, Ben and Margaret Mondics, Stanley and Golda Johnson, Charles and Jean Crider, the Henderson sisters, and Gordon and Evelyn Zytkoskee. Do you know any of them?"

"Well, I went to school with Gordon's brother, and we taught Neal's brothers in Pathfinders. That's about it," Wayne responded pleasantly, trying to mask his perplexity over the switch in plans.

While Elder Bradley spoke casually of the modification in our language study program and mission field as if it were as simple as a choice between salad dressings, I was inwardly rebelling. I didn't want to hear what he had to say. I was still enamored with learning German and going to see my mother's homeland. I never had imagined going to the Middle East. I wasn't even sure where the Arab Lands were, nor did I care. I studied the floor.

"I sense that the alteration in plans is a disappointment to you, Sister Olson," Elder Bradley said, noting the look of despondency clouding my face. "Why don't you two pray about it and give us your decision tomorrow. You are under no obligation to take the Arabic class or go to the Bible Lands. We can find another mission field for you. There are calls coming in every day."

Elder Bradley's understanding spirit lowered my resistance to his suggestion. I thought we should at least consider the possible change. We were still in a quandary as we left his office and headed for the seminary library. We got out the SDA yearbook and looked up the Middle East Union.

"Wow! Listen to this, Midge," Wayne exclaimed as he poured over the yearbook. "The population of the area is 93 million; the number of Seventh-day Adventists is only 1,300! That's a pathetic statistic! Furthermore, the encyclopedia says that about 95% of the people in the Middle East are Moslems. Imagine that! In the land where Christianity began, only 5% of the people are Christians. That's sad! They need missionaries." Wayne looked up at me meaningfully.

I could tell that Wayne's resistance to the change in mission fields had already crumbled. He continued to browse through the yearbook while I wandered over to the globe. I wanted to know just where in this world we might end up. My finger lingered on Germany for awhile, and then it drifted over to the eastern end of the Mediterranean Sea. There they were—the Bible lands! Almost halfway around the globe from my native South Dakota.

ARABIC ! ?

Wayne walked over to me. "Well, I don't know about you, Midge, but I'm convinced that we should go to the Middle East. If we are willing to go as missionaries, we ought to be willing to go where we are needed the most."

What could I say? Silently I examined my motives for mission service. I had wanted to see my mother's German homeland and learn her native tongue. Suddenly that seemed wrong. It made me seem like a self-serving person rather than a self-sacrificing missionary. Going to the Middle East where I didn't want to go would be to sacrifice my personal interests. Within my honest soul, I knew I should be led by His spirit rather than my desires. I didn't want to be a Jonah—choosing my own mission field rather than "Ninevah".

We went home and prayed the submissive prayer of Isaiah, "Here am I, Lord, send me." When we arose from our knees, we were impressed that God had pointed us to the Bible Lands and were satisfied with His decision.

On Monday morning we went to our first Arabic class. Elder George Keough, veteran missionary to upper Egypt, greeted us with "Salaam alaikum." Translated it meant "peace to you (plural)." Immediately I knew that a good old American "hello" was much simpler, but I promised myself that I would learn Arabic. The real surprise came when our teacher wrote our names on the chalkboard in Arabic. He wrote from the RIGHT to the LEFT in a script completely different from our Latin letters. It looked like lines and humps and dots to me. By comparison, it made shorthand appear elementary.

Elder Keough was a patient teacher with an I.Q. and wisdom that probably rivaled Solomon's. He worked tirelessly with us, trying to get us to roll our R's and cough out the guttural sounds correctly. About the time we all had tied tongues and sore throats, he smiled and said, "Don't be discouraged if Arabic doesn't come easily. The European languages are simple because they all stem from Latin and are, therefore, really not foreign languages to the English-speaking person." (He probably knew some of most of the European languages.) "Greek was harder for me to learn, but Arabic was the most difficult of all. It took me two years to master it."

"Give me 10 years," I groaned, looking at the flashcards I held in my hand scrawled in the Arabic script. On the back of each card I had written phonetically in Latin letters how the word should be pronounced in Arabic and its meaning in English. I couldn't trust my Arabic script nor my memory.

"Oh, you'll learn it, Mildred," Elder Keough said, smiling broadly. "You are the curious sort. You'll learn it so you'll know what's going on."

I looked at him quizzically, not knowing whether he meant that as a criticism or a compliment. But I liked Elder Keough, and his assessment of me was right. I smiled and let it go.

We learned a lot more than Arabic from Elder Keough. He taught us what mission service and sacrifice was all about. He pioneered the work in upper Egypt, and his experiences there would have filled volumes. He also knew the Bible better than anyone else we had met. We became such avid Keough disciples that we went to his home every Friday night to listen to his lectures on the book of Revelation.

One day in class Elder Keough told us how he had delivered their second baby at home in the most primitive of conditions. With a grocery string he tied the cord and cut it with his wife's garden scissors. We were aghast. This stimulated a this-won't-happen-to-us mentality among us. A little more than nine months later, three of us six couples had babies delivered by Dr.

ARABIC ! ?

Hughes at the Washington Sanitarium and Hospital. Our baby was born July 20, and we named her Ronnalee Gayle. The nurses put a bow in her long, dark hair and carried Ronnie around the hospital with them. She was their little pet.

In those days, mothers and babies were kept in the hospital for 10 days. At the end of that time, Ronnalee and I checked out to go home. I hated to take the most beautiful and best-natured baby ever to occupy the San's nursery away from the nurses, but they would just have to relinquish our bundle of sunshine to share with the rest of the world.

Our Arabic class ended in July, and we mission appointees attended the 1946 General Conference Session held in the Sligo Church in Takoma Park. By that time all but one family of our Arabic class had calls: Pogues to the Far East, Rowes to Egypt, Osters to Iran (where he had grown up), and Moles and us to Lebanon. The afternoon of our dedication to mission service, we dressed up in Arab garb and sang a song in Arabic. We didn't know the meaning to all the words in the song yet, but we could read the Arabic script. (Arabic words are pronounced as they are spelled—no silent letters or exceptions to the rule like in English.)

As we knelt in dedication, I squeezed a tear or two from my eyes. I felt humbled before God and desired, more than anything else in the world, to serve Him. Then God's presence seemed to envelop me like a warm, comforting cloak. The sacred service left me trembling.

When the dedication service was over, I searched the audience for my mother. My eyes zeroed in on that saintly soul who had taught me the scriptures daily, instilled in me a love for God, and inspired me to devote my life to His service. I had often marveled at her patience with me—the Katzenjammer Kid. How could she ever hope that her blond, mischievous tom-boy would turn out to be God's kid! No matter what I did, my parents and my church family had never given up on me. I noted that Mom's handkerchief made several trips to her eyes, and I knew that tears of joy were satisfying her soul as she saw another of her children join God's foreign mission army.

When the General Conference Session was over, we took another series of physicals, completed our dental work, got our passports, applied for visas and work permits, and bought and packed our goods for shipping. We had not expected it would take two months to complete these tasks; we were relieved when the preparations were over. Then we left our goods in the care of the General Conference Transportation Agency and drove West to tell our families goodbye. Our term of service was six consecutive years with no furloughs—a long, long stretch for those of us who came from closely-knit families. But separations were one of the sacrifices mission service entailed.

The General Conference men told us we would have several months to visit relatives while they worked on our papers. We spaced our time and spent a few days with each sibling except Lela, of course, who was already in Brazil.

We spent Thanksgiving with Wayne's family in Oregon. Then we journeyed back to South Dakota to be with my family for Christmas.

The middle of January the telegram arrived: "You sail January 30 aboard the Marine Carp. Proceed New York January 26."

Though we had been expecting this message, the finality of it hit us all quite hard, especially my sister Dorathy. She had come to Washington when Ronnie was three weeks old and had taken care of her while

ARABIC ! ?

Wayne and I completed the necessary preparations for departing the United States. Then Dorathy made the entire circuit West with us as we visited relatives. She had literally been Ronnie's nanny for five months, Now she would have to part with the baby to whom she had become very emotionally attached. She cried and carried Ronnie with her everywhere during our last days on the farm.

The day for us to board the train for New York arrived. No parting was ever more traumatic for anyone than this one was for Dorathy. I almost felt guilty taking "her baby" from her. As our train pulled away from the station in Sioux Falls, I looked back to see Dorathy weeping uncontrollably. And I knew the pain she felt; I was suffering too.

CHAPTER 3

SHIP AHOY, AND ALL THAT STUFF

It took two days and a night on the train to reach New York. From the depot we took a cab to the hotel and settled in. We had only two days in the Big Apple to complete our shopping list and see the sights. The immensity of New York City, its cosmopolitan atmosphere, and its maze of skyscrapers left us country kids breathless.

With a map in hand, we raced around the city trying to complete the necessary details and to squeeze in time for the sites—Radio City, the Empire State Building, Times Square, Wall Street, and other famous spots. Little Ronnie ate and napped on the go. The last night, on impulse, I bought a beautiful chestnut-colored, lamb skin coat from a street vendor. The combed and brushed, two-inch thick wool imitated fine fur. Of course, it would not have deceived a fur connoisseur, but it made me feel like the Queen of Sheba. I loved caressing its irresistible softness and feeling the comfort of it's cuddly warmth. Though it was inexpensive, it looked great and turned out to be the smartest purchase of my lifetime.

Thursday morning arrived, cold and misty—sort of like my drooping spirits. My lack of appetite was probably caused by the knots in the pit of my stomach. Wayne ate his last breakfast from the snacks in our room. (We lived frugally since we didn't know about expense reports.) We took our last cab ride to the sea port. We walked our last steps on American soil and boarded our ship, the Marine Carp. Maybe it wouldn't be our last of everything, but at that moment, I felt I was stepping into eternity.

The Marine Carp had been a troop ship during the war and had not yet been converted into a passenger liner. There was so much demand for transportation into the Mediterranean area during those first few months following World War II, that ship owners could operate almost any kind of tub and get business. Most of the passengers were people from the Eastern Mediterranean countries—Egypt, Greece, Syria, Lebanon, and Palestine—going back to see their families and homelands. The unsuspecting passengers did not realize how dearly they had paid for sub-standard transportation until they saw their cabins. Then they were angry, but there were no refunds on their tickets. The Marine Carp was only a carrier at best. There were no luxuries, no amenities, no comforts—not even a passengers' lounge. It was just a bare-bones, troop ship. The cabins were dismal. They had steel gray, metal walls with only a few hooks on which to hang one's clothing. Suitcases stashed under the beds served as dresser drawers. But I didn't mind any of this; if the troops could travel this way, so could I. I was a novice in world travel and, therefore, had no expectations for the common comforts of ocean voyages as did the experienced passengers.

I stood at the ship's railing holding baby Ronnie and watching the drama unfolding on the dock. Some partings seemed to be the happy, temporary ones, while others were the sad, goodbye-forever kind. Then I watched the crew reel up the gangplank, and I felt the ship's engines vibrate. Suddenly a wave of desperation swept over me as I realized that I was about to leave my country. Dread, fear, loneliness, and dejection

SHIP AHOY, AND ALL THAT STUFF

enveloped me—I thought I would burst with emotion. Just then Wayne joined me at the railing.

"Well, ship ahoy and all that stuff," I said, trying to hide behind a facade of nonchalance. I hoped he wouldn't notice the tremor in my voice. "Where have you been?"

"Down saving people's suitcases," Wayne responded, oblivious to my trauma. "Do you know, Midge, I have never seen such deplorable irresponsibility. I went down to pick up our suitcases as they came off the conveyor belt onto the ship's deck from the dock. Two stevedores stood there grabbing the suitcases and literally throwing them against the side of the ship, purposely trying to break them open. When they succeeded, it was difficult to tell how much they stuffed into their sacks and how much they put back into the suitcases. So I got in there, caught as many of the suitcases as I could, and set them aside. Then other passengers joined me in the suitcase relay. Our help was not appreciated. I am concerned that careless handling of the passengers' possessions is indicative of the service we can expect on this ship."

As it turned out, Wayne's observation was more prophetic than we imagined.

Then the ship was moving. Suddenly I wished someone from my church would have been there to see us off. I envied a young Presbyterian couple, also bound for Beirut, who were surrounded by a bevy of their church members. It seemed that everyone except me was holding paper streamers connecting them with family or friends on the dock. As the ship gradually moved farther from land, the streamers broke, symbolizing the severed connection between those leaving and those left behind. We stood alone by the railing experiencing our own separation anguish.

MIDGE IN LEBANON

As the little tugboats pushed our ship out into the harbor, I tried to push away the despondency gripping my heart. No longer could I control my emotions. Large lumps in my throat threatened to choke me. Tears streamed down my cheeks as the Statue of Liberty faded from my view. I thought of my mother who, 43 years earlier, had seen that same lady as her ship sailed INTO New York harbor. Perhaps some of the same anxieties smothered her—fear of the unknown, homesickness, and the pain of remembering the family left behind. I wondered if I would ever see that statue again, or if I would be one to make the ultimate sacrifice. Had I known the dangers that lurked in our future, I may never have left America at all. God, in His mercy, hid the future from our view. By faith we sailed into our impending destiny.

Soon we were out of the harbor, and the little tugboats left us. As we headed for the open sea the thrill of our new adventure captivated me. I was through feeling despondent. I had always wanted to be a missionary; now I was on my way to my mission field. Surely there could be no greater satisfaction than having my dreams fulfilled. I entered mission service with the same gung-ho enthusiasm that was so much a part of my nature.

The next order of business was to get settled into our cabins for the 14-day ocean voyage. Wayne was escorted to a tiny inside cabin which he would share with five other men. It was then we passengers learned that we would live dormitory style and use the dirty, communal bathrooms at the end of the long gangways. Beside these inconveniences, the ship was cold. Now I was very

thankful for my lambskin coat; I could tuck Ronnie inside of it too, keeping both of us cuddly warm.

SHIP AHOY, AND ALL THAT STUFF

We finally located my lazy cabin steward who had probably been hiding out somewhere. At this point we were still very trusting novices, and we didn't suspect him of any foul play. When we met him, he made such a convincing pretense of being concerned for my welfare that we almost thanked the "gods" for our good fortune in having him as my steward.

When the wily steward unlocked the door to the small but nice outside cabin to which I had been assigned, he exclaimed in alarm, "Oh, no! You don't want THIS cabin!"

"Why not?" I asked innocently, falling into his trap.

"Because it is near the bow. This ship has no ballast in the bottom to keep it from bobbing around like a cork in the open seas. This is too dangerous for you and the baby. You will get SICK TO DEATH here."

Then he turned to Wayne, who was almost invisible under his burden of Ronnie's buggy and paraphernalia, and practiced his saintly charm. "I'll tell you what I'll do, Mr. Olson. For $15 1 will make a switch. I'll put your wife and baby in a much larger cabin in the middle of the ship where they will be safer, warmer, and more comfortable."

Then he waited for our reaction. Being the innocents that we were, we quickly agreed to his plan. In fact, we thanked him profusely and handed over the cash. How could we know that this devious man was contriving to get as many of the women as possible into one large cabin so that he would have fewer cabins to clean. Now, instead of being in a nice cabin with two ladies, he herded me into a large, outside cabin with six other ladies and two small children. Only the bunk above mine was empty. I piled a lot of my extra baggage there while Wayne proceeded to lash Ronnie's buggy to my bunk.

MIDGE IN LEBANON

My "amiable" steward turned into a demon. "Here! You can't do that!" he shouted angrily. "The baby has to sleep in the bunk with her mother."

Wayne tried to reason with the man for sometime, but he continued his tirade. At last the stubborn Swede in Wayne surfaced. Calmly but decidedly Wayne told him, "Move out of my way. My baby will sleep in the buggy tied to her mother's bed. It is far safer than for the two of them to sleep in one narrow bunk as you suggest. If we cannot agree on my plan, I will seek help from your superiors."

Immediately the steward acquiesced, regained his sanity, and left. We were amazed at his sudden change of behavior. How could we know that the steward wanted to avoid, at all costs, someone of higher rank checking up on him? Experience with this character taught us to be much wiser travelers.

The first few days out of New York we hit a storm that just wouldn't quit. Whenever the boat hit a swell or a trough, the suitcases stashed under the bunks scooted across the floor. Only the very agile person could leap out of the pathway of those flying missiles in time to keep from being maimed. Almost everyone stayed in bed—either for safety's sake or because they were seasick. The stench of vomit permeated the rooms, gangways, and bathrooms. The stewards themselves were too sick to clean up the messes, so they threw down sawdust to absorb the moisture. Outside of a few ship workers, the only person I saw moving about, besides myself and Ronnie, was an old Greek man.

I carried Ronnie up to the dining room, but no one was there to serve us food. They had wet the table cloths, but even then the dishes wouldn't stay on the table because the ship was rolling and tossing so violently.

SHIP AHOY, AND ALL THAT STUFF

There was no smell of food cooking—either the cooks were sick too or the pans wouldn't stay on the stove.

One pallid waiter sat at a table handing out soda crackers and apples. I managed to stay on my chair while I ate, but the old Greek man wasn't so lucky. Then I took some food down to Wayne and his room mates, all of whom were miserably sick.

"I brought you guys some crackers," I said cheerily. "They tell me they are just the thing for seasickness."

"Please go away, Midge," Wayne moaned. "I can't stand the sight of food."

"But, Wayne," I teased, "you need this green apple to match that most interesting shade of green in your face."

"You aren't funny," Wayne replied, groaning some more. "It absolutely makes me dizzy watching the clothes hanging on the hook sway from side to side. Now I am convinced that all jokes about seasickness are cruel."

About then one of his roommates leaped out of bed and headed for the bathroom. Another man just leaned over his upper bunk and let it splatter on the floor. That was all the incentive I needed to leave. Besides, the stench in the ship was sufficiently nauseating to make a well person ill.

In desperation, I decided to go up on deck for a breath of clean air. It was a challenge to negotiate the steps—one minute they were horizontal and with the next roll of the ship, they were perpendicular.

I stood in the middle of the deck clutching my baby and trying to stay upright. Suddenly a big wave came rolling over the deck. The force of it knocked me right off my feet and onto my back. I slid toward the edge of the deck and was afraid I was going to go overboard. "Please Lord, save me," I prayed.

MIDGE IN LEBANON

I pressed my heels as hard as I could on the deck, hoping to stop my descent. I squeezed Ronnie tightly in my arms. She seemed to sense my fear and struggled to free herself. "Dear God," I prayed, "don't let her get away from me."

About that time the ship rolled the other direction, but I moved very little. I still laid on my back pushing on the deck with my heels, trying to maneuver myself over to the steps. Ronnie was crying and I was praying.

"Get down below deck!" a sailor shouted . "It's dangerous up here."

"I know," I yelled back. "Help me get to the steps, PLEASE!"

"Lord Almighty, if you don't have a baby with you too!" he exclaimed, not sacrilegiously. He pulled me by my lambskin coat over to the steps and took Ronnie from my arms. Then I was able to pull myself up to the stair rail and walk down the steps. He followed me down the steps and handed Ronnie back to me. "Now, Madame, get to your cabin and stay there until the storms dies down."

I took his advice.

The next day dawned clear and beautiful. About half of the passengers were up. As we passed through the Gulf Stream flowing northward, Wayne, Ronnie, and I stood at the rail watching the flying fish and the iridescent sea weed. Now this was my idea of ocean travel—soft rolling waves, salty spray, and sea life. Though other passengers were dissatisfied with the ship and its crew, we were blissfully happy because we had never known the comforts of a luxury liner.

About nine days out of New York, we passed through the Straits of Gibraltar. We were captivated by the dolphins that played around our ship. We raced from

SHIP AHOY, AND ALL THAT STUFF

one side of the ship to the other, seeing Spain off to our left and North Africa off to our right. It was wonderful to see land again.

The Mediterranean Sea was surprisingly calm and blue, and the warm sunshine drew everyone from their dingy cabins up onto the deck. As for the Olsons, we had been exploring the ship from stem to stern ever since Wayne had gotten his sea legs. All three of us became regular "old salts." The cold Atlantic Ocean breezes hadn't bothered us because Ronnie and I kept toasty warm in my sheepskin coat, and Wayne was comfortable in his long underwear and overcoat. Now that we were in the warm Mediterranean, I had to exchange my cherished fur for a sweater. Without my lambskin, I didn't feel like a fancy lady anymore.

The day before we were to land in Beirut, we packed our suitcases carefully in preparation for disembarking. I was getting quite anxious to see the country that would be my home for the next six years. I was hoping someone would be there to meet us because I was sure I couldn't remember enough Arabic to get me where I needed to go.

Early the next morning Wayne, Ronnie, and I were out on the deck straining our eyes to catch our first glimpse of Lebanon. In the distance we sighted the beautiful Lebanon Mountain range covered with the unique umbrella pines. Soon we could see white-washed, stone houses with red tile roofs dotting the hillsides. With binoculars we could see the banana, date, and citrus fruit trees that grew along the sea coast. As we steamed closer to the shore, cars and people became distinguishable.

The day was February 13, 1947. Back in South Dakota it was still warm coat and mitten weather; here, I was even too warm in my winter dress. I dashed back to the cabin, pulled off my woolen dress, and donned my new black silk. "There, that should make a good impression," I told Ronnalee. She smiled and cooed amiably while I dressed her in half socks and a red-checked gingham dress. "Now we are ready to meet whoever is kind enough to come after us. The telegram said someone would be here," I said as I picked Ronnie up from the bunk.

We waited on the deck as our ship pulled up to the dock. Many of the passengers came to kiss Ronnie, "the ship's happy baby", goodbye and wish us well. Ronnalee had captivated their hearts and brought shafts of sunlight into the lives of many of the passengers during the dreary days on the Atlantic. Her friendly nature had helped us be missionaries on the ship; now we were to become missionaries for real in a foreign country.

Wayne scanned the hundreds of people waiting on the dock. "I think I see some folks that might have come to meet us," he remarked.

"I hope you are right!" I added anxiously.

The greeting we received, however, totally overwhelmed us.

CHAPTER 4

EXCITEMENT IN BEIRUT

"Olsons? OLSONS!" someone was calling from the dock.

We peered over the edge of the railing. "We're the Olsons," Wayne yelled back. Then the 20 or more people who had gathered on the dock to meet us waved back. "We'll meet you at the end of the gangplank," someone shouted.

Wayne and I were overwhelmed at the size of the welcoming committee. "Can you believe that!" Wayne exclaimed, still agape at the pleasant surprise. "No one to see us off in New York, but a whole crowd here."

"Oh, I love these people already," I said impulsively. "I can't wait to get better acquainted."

Wayne rushed down to my cabin and started dragging Ronnalee's things and mine up on the deck while I stood guard over our stuff. As usual, Ronnalee was being passed from one passenger to the next for another round of kisses and enjoying every minute of it.

The ship was scarcely moored to the dock before porters started swarming onto the still-not-secured gangplank and the deck. I was both stunned and alarmed by their aggressiveness. I had never before seen anyone so forceful, and I worried that they would steal us blind. I snatched Ronnie away from an old Greek grandma and held her tightly. But not tightly enough, evidently. The next thing I knew a turbined Kurdish porter had wrested her out of my arms. Then he took off holding Ronnie under one arm and three suitcases in the other.

"Wait!" I screamed. "Don't run off with my baby."

In my distress, I turned to the ship's purser. "Follow him, Madame," he advised.

I did—at a pace that should have required a new entry in the Guiness book!

"He's got my baby," I cried to the first American missionary standing dose enough to the gangplank to hear.

"Don't worry," Mr. King (who I later learned was our mission treasurer) called back. "He's only trying to help. Follow him into customs house. Wayne and I will meet you there later."

Follow him? That was easy for Mr. King to say. My sea legs caused me to stagger like a drunkard, and fear that the porter was kidnapping my baby didn't help either. When I stumbled into the customs house, there was the porter. He set Ronnie and the suitcases down on the counter. "Know number," he smiled, pointing to a number pressed into a metal tag he wore on his shirt. Then he raced back to the ship to find Wayne.

I was relieved to have Ronnie in my arms again but was scandalized to see what I had carried off the ship with me—my lambskin coat, Ronnie's diaper bag, a hatbox (not mine), a vanity case (not mine), and an umbrella (not mine). In my frenzy I had just latched onto anything handy. Within the next hour we got everything back to its rightful owners. Mrs. King came into the customs house and assured me that what looked like chaos to us worked effectively for them. She said that the porters were honest and necessary—a big help in

EXCITEMENT IN BEIRUT

speeding our landing process. I began to breathe normally again but not for long.

It had been previously decided that Ronnie and I would go home with Mrs. King by taxi to Mouseitbe, a suburb of Beirut. Mr. King and Khalil would help Wayne get our trunks through customs. We didn't have much—most of our possessions were still in the warehouse in New York and would follow on a freighter later.

After greeting the Lebanese Adventists and the mission families on the dock, Mrs. King, Ronnie, and I climbed into an old Model A Ford taxi. I hadn't seen anything so antique outside of a museum and was quite thrilled that I would get to ride in a genuine Model A. The "thrill", as in rapt pleasure, lasted only until we got out of the port area. Then the taxi driver put his left hand out of the window and squeezed the bulb of his squawk horn. He wasn't just kidding either. He gunned the engine which threw us back into our seats. He scattered the pedestrians like flocks of chickens as animated bodies leaped with alacrity to either side of the narrow, winding streets. I closed my eyes as I held onto Ronnie with one hand and the door post with the other. "Please don't kill anyone, Sir," I squeaked through tightened vocal cords. "Blood makes me faint."

"Yes, yes. Nice day," the driver answered in broken English, not understanding a word I was saying. And you can bet that, with my brain frozen in fear, I couldn't think of the Arabic word for "slow down."

Then I remembered the word for God. "Allah," I breathed aloud, "I need your help."

The driver was obviously pleased with my one-word Arabic vocabulary. "Nam, Allah, ho al akbar." (Yes, God is great) Then he floor-boarded the gas peddle again to the next totally blind intersection where he slammed on the brakes and squawked his horn some more. I guess he figured if both he and I believed in Allah we were invincible.

The harrowing ride jostled us up and down, to and fro, and back and forth which caused us to do considerable traveling inside the car as well. I had no idea that a Model A had such get-up-and-go in it. Whenever we left a crossing, we were thrown back against our seats. Then, when we neared a cross street, he slammed on the brakes so hard that only my knees pressing firmly against the front seat kept me from joining the driver.

Somewhere in the middle of town, the driver slid to a screeching halt. I opened my eyes to see a crowd of people gathered around a body lying on the street. After some men completed a brief inspection of it, they dragged the man's body off to the side of the street by his arms, leaving his feet to bounce loosely over the cobble stones.

"Wh—what happened?" I asked the driver as a chill swept over me. "Someone couldn't jump fast enough? Got hit by a taxi? Is he dead? What? WHAT?"

The taxi driver muttered something in colloquial Arabic which I did not understand. I didn't understand classical Arabic, either, for that matter. And I didn't understand WHY I had ever put foot in that taxi.

I looked over at Mrs. King. Other than holding onto the door post, she sat placidly composed, oblivious to this whole scary experience.

Then Mrs. King glanced my way and noted my terror. "Don't worry," she said, patting my arm. "That man may have been killed, or he may have died of natural causes, or he may have just passed out from this unusually hot winter day, or, or something else."

EXCITEMENT IN BEIRUT

I blinked my eyes. I couldn't believe her pragmatism; she accepted this wild taxi ride and the man lying on the street as if it were the norm. If this was an ordinary day in Lebanon, I wagered that I'd soon be wearing a straight jacket on my way back to the states.

"Aren't you afraid of this man's driving?" I gasped. "It's worse than New York."

"Oh, no," Mrs. King laughed. "Lebanese are excellent drivers. They almost never have accidents. Machines were made for Arabs. They take naturally to anything scientific or mechanical. I'm very comfortable with their skills."

"I'm not!" I stated honestly. "I haven't made out a will. My debts can go to anyone who wants them but remember that my baby should go to my sister Dorothy."

Mrs. King smiled. "You'll get used to it and love it. Lebanon and Lebanese are marvelous. You're just having a little culture shock."

Culture shock? So that's what they called the fears I had been through since our boat docked. Shock? I could agree. Culture? I questioned.

After the longest half-hour ride of my life, we arrived at the mission house safely. The taxi driver stepped out, opened my door, and gallantly helped me out of his cab. While my legs threatened to buckle under me, the charming smile of the driver disarmed me, and I liked the friendliness I saw in his face. I began to think that he wasn't a bad sort after all. I stretched my benevolence even farther. After the 14-day ship voyage, my blood pressure probably needed some stimulation. Between him and the aggressive porter, they had succeeded marvelously in doing that. Maybe that was good.

In front of the mission house, I met the Ghazal families. The men were Adventist building contractors who, judging by their comfortable homes, evidently did well at their profession. The Ghazals were warm and friendly people, and I liked them immediately. I knew we would become good friends.

It was not until I got up into Kings' second floor apartment that I realized the back of my dress was torn from the waist down to the hem. Evidently a spring had popped through the aging leather seat covering of the taxi and had snagged my dress and slip. I was horrified to think that the Ghazals must have seen my under garments as I walked up the steps to Kings' apartment. I wondered why I hadn't felt a draft of air through the rip—that would have alerted me to my immodest condition. Perhaps I was still too numb with "culture shock" to notice.

Mrs. King and I sat down on the davenport and had a hearty laugh. Then I took my suitcase into the bedroom and changed. The dress was unsalvageable.

About noon, Wayne and Mr. King came from the port. The customs officials had been most gracious and hurried the process along. Wayne was gloating over the fact that he could already count in colloquial Arabic. Furthermore, he had enjoyed a relaxed ride in a Model A across town. Obviously his taxi driver and mine had not taken driver's education from the same teacher. (After I had lived in Lebanon a few months, I had to agree with Mrs. King—the Lebanese were good drivers. My first taxi ride was the most frightening one of all, and never again did I see a body in the streets.)

During lunch, Mrs. King told us about customs and foods in Lebanon. "Lebanon, like Palestine, is also 'a land flowing with milk and honey.' Post-war prices, however, make us pay dearly for milk, honey, bread, and other commodities. Cost of living has caused us to change our American eating habits. We have adopted Lebanese cuisine. It is very nutritious and delicious."

After sampling the Lebanese food, I liked it immediately. I would have no trouble adapting to the Lebanese diet.

In the evening, Bob Mole, our good friend from our seminary Arabic class, came to take us to their apartment in Beit Meri, the mountain village where Middle East College was quartered for the winter. As he drove the 15 miles up the narrow, winding road (which had no guard rails) in the school's old panel truck, he regaled us with sensational tales he had heard that happened both before and after his arrival.

"Right here," he said, pointing to a small crater in the middle of the road, "was where they tried to blow up a member of parliament last week. The timing device was off a bit, however, so the bomb only got his tail pipe." Bob chortled as if it were a joke. Wayne, pretending to be a good listener, attempted a little chuckle. I, sitting in the windowless back end of the panel truck near the tail pipe, wasn't the least bit amused. I was sprouting a good case of goose bumps. Bob had no idea what he was doing to my psyche as he continued to tell about bandits stopping cars and robbing the passengers.

I abhorred Bob's Chicago-like crime bulletins. "Isn't there any law here?"

"Yes, but you see," Bob proceeded to philosophize, "Lebanon and Syria were both French mandates after World War I, and they have only recently gained independent status. They have organized their own systems of government and are doing an admirable job of establishing democratic nations. They'll have things under control soon. Anyway, we feel very safe here in Lebanon. In just the two months we've lived here, we've learned to love Lebanon and its people. The only

MIDGE IN LEBANON

disadvantage we feel is unheated houses and a limited variety of food. But the Lebanese are real entrepreneurs; I suspect they'll soon be producing a great variety of fruits and vegetables. They've got the land to do it and the right climate—coastal, sub-tropical and mountain temperate."

Within two years Bob's prediction proved true. In the meantime we learned to live on cabbage, cauliflower, citrus fruit, beans, lentils, bananas, bread, and rice. It wasn't a bad diet for adults but a little rough for my six-month old baby.

It was dark and cold when we arrived at the mountain hotel, temporary campus for Middle East College. The dim lights seemed to cast ominous shadows and a strange foreboding engulfed us. Before the night was over, we would experience sheer terror!

CHAPTER 5

THE LONG DREADFUL NIGHT

When we arrived in Lebanon in February, 1947, Middle East College operated out of temporary rented quarters in the mountain village of Beit Meri. The next year faculty and students anticipated being on their own "new earth", as they lovingly dubbed the 70-acre mountain property the mission had purchased in a suburban area five miles east of Beirut. The Hassos of Iraq had provided the money; Arthur Keough and the mission officers had made the purchase; and the Ghazals were already constructing two stone dormitory buildings on the site.

The college itself was the brain child of Elder George Keough, our Arabic teacher. For years, Elder Keough had maintained that the secret to the progress of missions anywhere was to train talented, indigenous youth for the task. Under his prodding, the Adventist College of Beirut was established in 1939 in a portion of our Mouseitbe elementary/secondary school with Arthur Keough, son of George, as principal. A dozen young men attended the two-year training classes offered for Adventist ministers and teachers. Wartime conditions in Lebanon forced the school to move to Amman, Jordon, for a year; then it returned to the Beirut area permanently. By 1944, the enrollment overflowed the available space in Mouseitbe; subsequently, the board moved the college into larger, temporary quarters until the mission could build its own facility.

MIDGE IN LEBANON

The easy life-style of Middle East people made a rental solution for this problem relatively simple. During the warm summer, people from all over the Middle East customarily spent extended vacations in the comfortable hotels of the cool, dry mountains of lovely Lebanon; but in the nine months of winter, these luxury hotels were vacant. So during the winter, Middle East College rented a large hotel and some additional apartment buildings in Beit Meri at a nominal cost. It was an ideal set-up except for one thing—there was no heat in the hotels and no stoves in the country to be purchased. Little kerosene heaters could raise the temperature a few degrees, but they also polluted the air. Though the days were usually semi-warm and sunny, the nights were frigid. Much of the time the faculty and students had to wear their coats and sweaters.

The night we arrived at Hotel Ghassoub, I raced up the steps into the arms of my good friend, Jeannette. She, Bob, and two-year-old Annette lived in the hotel manager's summer apartment which occupied the front portion of the second floor of the hotel. It was here that we spent our first dreadful night.

The night began very well. Expatriate workers came by to meet us—Harders (F.E.J. was the college president), Norrises (he was business manager), teachers Edith Davis, Shahin Ilter, and Ben and Margaret Mondics. After they left, we settled down in Moles' living room to unwind from the day's excitement. Bob, however, had still not exhausted his repertoire of sensational stories. He filled our bedtime story hour with more horror tales. As we crawled into bed that night, we were well primed for the worst scenario. We were not disappointed!

Wayne and I shivered together and discussed the day's events while we warmed up the bed. We were so

THE LONG DREADFUL NIGHT

tense we had difficulty in dropping off to sleep. We finally caught a few winks before a fracas outside of our bedroom window sent us into orbit.

"Wh—what was THAT?" I whispered. "It sounds like someone crying or, or groaning, or..." I was interrupted by rattling, banging noises, and growl-like sounds.

Wayne sprang out of bed and ran to the window to investigate. "It looks like a bunch of small dogs having a midnight snack from the garbage can they just dumped over. I can tell they haven't been to Sabbath School—they know nothing about sharing."

I didn't think Wayne was very witty, but I was relieved that he could explain the reason for the scrimmage. After Bob's scary stories, I was expecting a murder per night up here in the mountains, and that is exactly what I thought was happening outside of our window. It sounded like someone crying for help and putting up a good fight in the meantime.

We laughed about our groundless fears. Even so, it took us a LONG time to get back to sleep.

CRASH! CLATTER!! RUMBLE!!! The explosive sounds at the front of the hotel reverberated throughout the whole building. Simultaneously Wayne and I leaped out of bed and quivered together in the middle of the room.

"What was that?" I asked, my hair standing at attention.

"Beats me!" Wayne answered. "Sounds like someone tearing off the security bars from the front door. Maybe I should have moved our two trunks inside the apartment last night instead of leaving them in the hallway for the convenience of the thieves."

Then Wayne crept out into the living room to face the enemy. I jumped back into bed and pulled the covers up over my head. Wayne examined the apartment door—it was intact. He peeked out into the hallway—our trunks were still there. He peered over the balcony at the hotel's front door—still locked. Since Wayne was unable to solve the mystery and there seemed to be no robbers in the vicinity, he came back to bed. We did not go back to sleep.

In the morning two sleepy newcomers sat with the Moles at the breakfast table.

"What's the matter? Didn't you sleep well?" Bob asked. "You look tired."

Wayne yawned, "Well, it's the entertainment you have around here at nights. When we finally got to sleep the dogs dumped over the garbage can and…"

"Oh, that's the jackals. They come every night and tip over the garbage cans to eat the cafeteria's left overs," Jeannette laughed.

I didn't even emit a ha—ha.

Wayne continued, "Then about four this morning someone tried to break down the front door of the hotel."

Bob nearly rolled off his chair laughing. I didn't see anything funny in an attempted break-in, so I waited until Bob could control himself long enough to explain that one.

"That was the baker opening his establishment for the day." Bob wiped tears from his eyes. "His shop is directly below our living room. Didn't you notice a big corrugated door pulled down and locked to the right of the hotel's front door when you came in last night?"

"No, I didn't!" I answered. "It was dark." It did seem to me that before we went to bed Bob could have alerted us to their nightly disturbances. We had suffered eight hours of agony bound to age us ten years.

THE LONG DREADFUL NIGHT

"Well," Bob said, I guess I should have warned you about those things, but we're so used to it we sleep right through it. Not to worry! Honestly, you're safer here in Lebanon than you are in the large cities of America..."

"But, those stories you told—the ones about..." I questioned.

"Aw, Midge," Bob laughed. "You know that news dispatchers don't broadcast the mundane—they specialize in the sensational. I thought I gave you an excellent orientation period last night."

"That you did, Bob, that you did," I groaned as I fell asleep in my chair.

And that first night proved to be the worst of all the rest of the 5,796 nights we would spend in Lebanon.

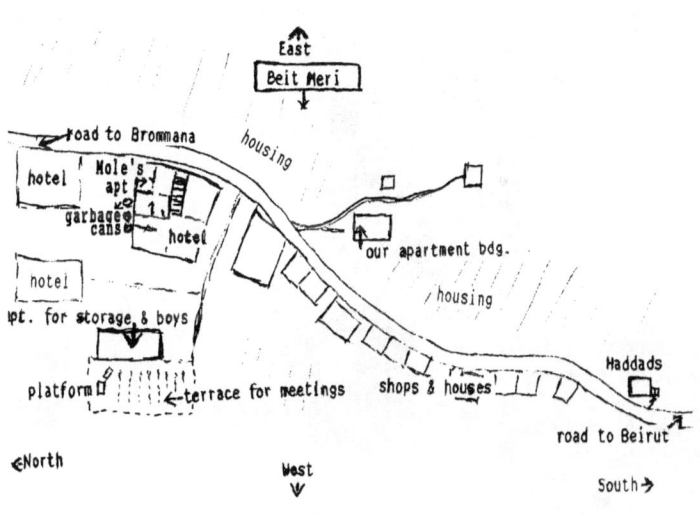

CHAPTER 6

HI HO, HI HO, IT'S OFF TO WORK WE GO

Elder E. L. Branson, the president of Middle East Union, came up to Beit Meri to see us. He had a warm smile that made us like him immediately.

"We're happy that you have joined our work force here in these challenging Bible Lands," he said. "We have a fine group of young workers here—both national and foreign. You'll blend right into the group."

We nodded.

"Now, Brother and Sister Olson," (this formal address made me feel a whole generation older) "we have had to change the plans we had for you." (Oh, no! Here we go again—a change in plans. Surely they won't shift us back to Germany after I've suffered through a year of Arabic lessons, I thought.) "Temporarily, that is." (Relief.) "We called you to pioneer the work in North Lebanon, but we feel it's too dangerous for you to go there at this time. They have just had a big riot in Tripoli between the Maronite Christians and the Moslems. There were about 16 people killed in the City Square. So until things cool down a bit, we do not think it is wise to send you up north." (He paused, and we waited for more.) "Now here are our revised plans. We thought you could stay right here at the college for awhile. Wayne, you could work with the students on construction down on the new earth. How does that sound?"

MIDGE IN LEBANON

What could we say? He knew more about the situation than we did, and we trusted his judgment. Wayne spread his hands. "Whatever you think is best."

Wayne went to work every day down on the new college property. Jeannette and I tended our babies and tried to create gourmet dishes with lentils, rice, beans, and cabbage. We didn't succeed, but the attempt kept us occupied.

We continued to live with the Mole family since our furniture and car hadn't as yet been shipped from America. After two months the weather warmed up; so we moved into two empty rooms of the apartment which the college had rented for a laundry. It wasn't ideal but it gave us a degree of independence. When summer came and the college closed for the school year, we rented the whole apartment. Then one happy day our furniture and car arrive. THAT was "Christmas" for the Olsons. I never had more fun opening my gifts at Christmas than I did tearing into those crates and barrels that I had packed ten months earlier.

It didn't take us long to get settled. We didn't have that much—Ronnie's chest, crib, and high chair, our bed and chest, a re-upholstered davenport, a rocking chair, four chairs and a dining table, a washing machine, fuel-oil heater, and a good kerosene cook stove with an oven. Since we had been sleeping on school cots, sitting on our trunks for chairs, using our suitcases as dresser drawers, and cooking on a one-burner primus, I now felt very rich. Other people thought we were rich because we owned one of the newest automobiles in Lebanon—a 1947, four-door Ford. We didn't bother to tell them that we owed Wayne's brother, Elmer, the whole cost of that luxury. The mission had advised us to bring a car with us since Wayne would need it in his ministerial work. It

HI HO, HI HO, IT'S OFF TO WORK WE GO

turned out to be good advise. That car became a real missionary vehicle.

The political situation in North Lebanon still had not stabilized by summer. The mission asked Wayne and me to hold an evangelistic effort in Beit Meri. I hired Mary Nessimian, a sweet Armenian girl, to take care of Ronnie so I would be free to make house calls with Wayne and play the organ for the evening meetings. Michael Kebbas and Yusif Fargo, two students from the college, were asked to assist us. All of us were in our early twenties. Why the mission entrusted us inexperienced young people with such an important work, I'll never know, but we jumped at the opportunity with all the enthusiasm of little leaguers. Ibrahim Swaidan, the college Arabic teacher and our translator for the summer, was the only mature one among us.

Perhaps it would be wise to explain something about the Arabic language at this point. All people of the Middle East, with the exception of Turkey, Iran, and Cyprus, speak their country's colloquial Arabic. Since the dialect spoken in each country varies, Arabs often prefer to communicate with one another in French or English. However, the classical Arabic is common to all Arab nations. That is the language used in the Koran, Bible, and all formal speeches. A sermon, for instance, should not be given in colloquial Arabic. Although Arabs understand and read their classical language, relatively few can speak it correctly. The grammar and word endings are very complicated.

At this time, neither Wayne nor I spoke enough Arabic to manage an ordinary conversation without the help of Michael or Yusif. (Eventually we became very conversant in colloquial Arabic. Most foreigners learn a few phrases but can't follow a conversation, or understand sermons or news broadcasts. We were happy when we finally learned to do both.)

We had no company of Adventist believers in Beit Meri upon which to build a congregation. After the college group left in June, the only Adventists remaining were our assistants, Yusif and Michael, Mary, the Swaidan family, Mrs. Haddad, a new convert, and Wayne and I. That didn't worry Wayne or me. We supposed that we would win a number of believers through the effort. We didn't know then that conversion of souls to the gospel in the Middle East comes extremely hard—one person at a time after months of study.

Michael, Yusif, Wayne and I began immediate preparations for the effort. First, we rented an open terrace behind one of the resort apartment buildings. It was a beautiful location for night meetings—a star-studded canopy above us and the twinkling lights of Beirut in the distant west below us. Since it doesn't rain in the Middle East from April until October, we were certain to have dry, comfortable, cool nights on our mountain terrace.

We rented the ground-floor apartment that led directly onto the terrace. In one room of the apartment we stored the hundred chairs we borrowed from the college for the summer; Michael and Yusif set up their bachelor quarters in the rest of the space. This close proximity to the terrace made it handy for the boys to guard the equipment, set it up, and take it down.

Next we put up poles and strung electrical wiring. We cleaned the stones and weeds off the terrace. We built a platform and fastened two sheets of plywood onto the back side on which we inscribed the ten commandments in Arabic. Last of all, we purchased an old pump organ, distributed our handbills, and prayed for God's blessing.

Sunday night came and so did the crowd. Most of the chairs were filled, and the audience gave good attention

HI HO, HI HO, IT'S OFF TO WORK WE GO

to the message. But the second night of our meetings a few young scalawags stood in the back and threw marble-size stones up to the front. As I played the organ, I was pelted with these missiles. The stones were unnerving—they hurt and distracted me. I had to keep flipping the stones off the keyboard. The stones disturbed Mr. Swaidan, the song leader and translator, as well as Wayne, the speaker. We endured the harassment that night but we surely did not want an encore. After the meeting we gathered in the boys' all-purpose room and prayed about it. We knew God had a solution for the problem; we only needed to discover what it was.

The next day we visited Mrs. Victoria Haddad. We needed the encouragement she had always given us. Mrs. Haddad was a conscientious Christian who had been baptized the previous winter after studying with some of the college students. Her three teenage children did not share her Adventist faith, and she did not force her convictions upon them. Anees, the 16-year old, had only recently recovered from a school bus accident that took the life of his friend. Perhaps Anees's miraculous deliverance prepared the family for what God had in mind for them.

Victoria and her daughter Mary attended our first meeting and were pleased that the audience seemed receptive to the message. The second night Victoria and Mary were there too, but they were disappointed with the village youth who threw stones to disrupt the meeting.

As we visited with Victoria in her home, she told us she had talked to her son Anees about the incident and that he would be at our next meeting. We didn't know then what that meant, but we soon found out. Perhaps it was out of respect for their mother's religion that Anees and Edmond attended our next meeting. Anees was only a teenager himself, but he had enough clout with his peers to subdue our antagonists. Anees's presence quelled all subversive activity and shamed the trouble makers into leaving. We had no more harassment the rest of the summer.

This experience in Beit Meri was only a prelude to what lay ahead for us. We often wished we had a young Anees to calm some of the bigger storms that we encountered later.

One Sunday we decided to use a novel and fast method for distributing our handbills. Since Middle East College president Harder and treasurer Norris owned airplanes parked down at the municipal airport, we asked them to fly over Brommana and Beit Meri and scatter our handbills. About noon, when the people were coming home from Sunday church services, Harder and Norris flew low over our mountain. Like the leaves of autumn, the handbills fluttered everywhere. Many of them ended up in the ravines and gullies for the goats and sheep to read, but enough landed on the streets to cause quite a sensation. Children, youth, and adults raced after the papers from heaven and read the message. We were thrilled with the effect. Harder and Norris, however, were not thrilled with what awaited them. When they landed at the airport, the police were there to take them into custody. They had flown low over the villages, dropping propaganda without official clearance to do so. The authorities were justified in taking the men into custody—a person should not flaunt the laws of the land just because he is an American. We sometimes tended to feel that we should be treated as VIP's because we carried an American passport. The countries of the Middle East were exceptionally good to us, but sometimes they had to draw the line, as they did in this case. Harder explained to the authorities that he meant no harm, presented them with a copy of the

HI HO, HI HO, IT'S OFF TO WORK WE GO

"propaganda" and proceeded to talk himself out of trouble. The Lebanese police were not fooled one bit by Harder's ploy, but in a gesture of good will, they let the men go. The next week we were back distributing our handbills the hard way—walking around town.

One Sunday night a very earnest young man, Edmond Shammas, came to the terrace. After the meeting he asked if he could study the subject of hell in more depth with us. We invited him to our home where we studied until two in the morning. Since it was so late, he stayed overnight with us. After breakfast we studied some more. It seemed there was no satisfying his thirst for Biblical knowledge. Initially he had come to the meeting because, as he said, "I picked up your handbill on the only subject I have been interested in for the past few years—HELL. I'm not worried about heaven, but I don't understand hell. No subject you could have presented would have enticed me as much, if at all. I'm from North Lebanon. I came down to Beirut Thursday to apply for a student visa to the United States. I stayed with friends in the village just below Beit Meri and was on my way back home when I chanced to find your advertisement on the subject of hell." (Was it chance or providence?) "I had to hear what you would say about it. Well, our studies have led us from one subject to another. Now I'm excited about all I've learned; I want my family to know this too."

"We'd like that too," Wayne assured him. "Why don't you stay here in Lebanon for another year and attend our Middle East College?"

"Your church has a COLLEGE?" Edmond questioned in astonishment. "I've never so much as heard of Seventh-day Adventists, and now you tell me your church is sufficiently established to run a college? Why haven't we in North Lebanon heard of Adventists before now?"

Wayne answered thoughtfully, "God willing, things will soon quiet down in North Lebanon, and we will move there to preach the gospel."

"Fantastic!" Edmond said enthusiastically. "I will introduce you to some of my friends and my family, and you can study with them."

Edmond was the key God provided for the message to enter North Lebanon. The handbill and the meeting with Edmond Shammas was not mere chance. God planned this rendezvous. If we had gone to North Lebanon as planned when we first arrived, we would not have met Edmond in Beit Meri nor have followed through the providential chain of events that ensued. We did not know God's master plan at this time, but He would reveal it to us a step at a time.

CHAPTER 7

FALLING IN LOVE

Edmond Shammas' two-day visit sparked anew the conviction that God had called us to carry the gospel to North Lebanon. Even before we left the states we felt drawn to this cause. Perhaps that is why we were somewhat disappointed when Elder Branson told us we could not go to North Lebanon immediately. God knew, however, that we needed the initiation period we were experiencing in Beit Meri to prepare us for what lay ahead. In those six months we fell in love with evangelism, the country, climate, and culture, the friends, food, and fun.

Among the first Lebanese to become our best friends were the Haddads—the mother, Victoria, and her children, Anees, 16, Mary, 14, and Edmond, 13. They were not wealthy people but they had class. Victoria's husband, an electrical engineer, had been killed in a work-related accident when the children were still small. In those days, there was no worker's compensation or insurance money to support the survivors; so Victoria's family stepped in and helped her raise the children. When Middle East College brought Adventism to Beit Meri, Victoria studied the message, accepted it, and was baptized. Since both the Haddad and Abdul-Messiah families were influential people in the community, it must have caused quite a stir in the village when Victoria courageously stepped out alone to become the first Seventh-day Adventist in Beit Meri. The fact that her relatives did not oppose nor desert her because of her decision, says something about the liberal mind-set of this family.

Victoria and her family could be justly proud of the job they had done in raising the three youngsters. The Haddad children were intelligent, ambitious, well-mannered, and fun-loving kids. They were highly motivated and energetic. Even as teenagers, they exhibited leadership qualities. We knew God could use these young people in His work and prayed for their conversion. On Saturday nights, the Haddad children, and Michael and Yusif often came to our house to play table games with Mary and us. On Sundays the same group, along with the Abou Jaoude children from Brommana, distributed handbills. Work and fun were equally pleasurable for us.

The hospitable Lebanese people reminded me of the people of mid-America where I had been raised. I felt comfortable among them. They often invited us to eat with them. These occasions were the highlights on our social calendar.

Mrs. Haddad introduced us to delectable Lebanese cuisine—hommos and tahini (pureed garbanzos mixed with olive oil, sesame seed butter, and fresh minced garlic), taboli (the world's most healthful salad made with parsley, mint, tomatoes, bulgur wheat, onions, lemon juice, and olive oil), kubeh (a meat, garbanzo, or potato dish made with bulgur wheat, seasonings, and onions patted about 1/2 inch thick into a pan, covered with olive oil, and baked in a hot oven), fatayer (spinach pie), baklava, etc.

Mary, Ronnie and I often went to the Haddads to watch Victoria make her mountain bread. How it turned out so perfectly round always amazed me. Victoria squeezed off a fistsize piece of bread dough, patted it a

FALLING IN LOVE

little flat, then tossed it in the air, manipulating it around and around with her hands until she got it cardboard thin. Then she flipped it onto a large, disklike, iron dome that was fiery hot from the fiercely-burning wood beneath it. The disk-like plate itself was set on top of ten-inch thick stones with an opening in front where Victoria deftly fed the fire and worked her bread at the same time. In two minutes Victoria peeled off the thin, 20-inch diameter bread sheet, delectably browned and nut-like tasty.

I thought there was nothing in the world as delicious as Mrs. Haddad's mountain bread rolled up with labni (like strained yogurt or cream cheese) and salty black olives inside of it. I soon learned that dibis (carob syrup) and tahini (sesame seed butter) were equally good inside of mountain bread—particularly when I was on a binge for sweets.

The feasts at the Abou Jaoudes' in Brommana were different in that they cooked deliciously flavored beans and French-fried potatoes over an open pit fire. I've never before nor since had potatoes that I liked as much. The Abou Jaoude boys, Salaam, Adul, and Habeeb, and the girls, Nassima, Najla, and Faiza always enticed us to over-eat of their good food.

We felt so comfortable with our Lebanese friends in these mountains that we never wanted to leave them. We suspected, however, that a move for us was in the offing. We didn't know when, but deep within our souls we knew where we should go—North Lebanon.

We were sorry when the summer was over and our meetings were finished. While we were waiting for our next assignment we decided to drive down to Palestine. On the Lebanese-Palestinian border, British peace-keeping forces examined our passports. They warned us that the Palestinian situation had become very tense since there were rumors of partitioning the country into Arab and Israel sectors. When we got to Jerusalem we saw what they meant—barricades were set up everywhere, and we were stopped frequently as we moved from one sector to another.

I was awed as we visited the Temple Mount, the Garden Tomb, Calvary, the Mount of Olives, the Upper Room, Bethlehem, Nazareth, and the Sea of Galilee. Seeing these sacred places connected with the life of Christ sent shivers down my back. But the most precious experience was my Thursday night vigil at the Garden of Gethsemane. Ten years earlier, at the South Dakota camp meeting, the Andersen brothers and my sister Lela and I had sung the song, "'Neath the Old Olive Trees." That song had stirred my soul to recommitment, and I knew intuitively that one day I would see the actual Garden of Gethsemane. Dick had ridiculed me when I said that one day I would kneel among those trees. Now I was here! My dream had become reality!

On the last Thursday night of August, 1947, we followed the path Jesus and his disciples had taken from the Upper Room, across the Kidron Valley, and into the garden. I wandered reverently along the pathways and among the olive trees, flowers, and stones. Some of the trees were over two thousand years old. Which ones had Jesus touched? Under which of those trees had He knelt? I moved to a gnarled old tree and dropped to my knees. The ground was damp and chilled from the evening dew. A full moon hovered just above the golden gate of the temple mount silhouetting the ancient eastern wall against the sky. The beauty of night and the sacredness of the place thrilled my soul. I sang softly the words of the song that had so touched my heart as a teenager:

FALLING IN LOVE

'Neath the shade of the night,
walked the Savior of light,
in a garden of dew-laden breeze.
Where no light could be found,
Jesus knelt on the ground,
there He prayed 'neath the old olive trees.
'Neath the old olive trees,
went the Savior alone on his knees.
'Not my will, Thine be done,'
cried the Father's own Son,
as He prayed 'neath the old olive trees.

My voice choked and I could no longer sing. In my mind's eye, I saw Jesus kneeling under one of these olive trees. He was praying for strength to endure the trial that awaited Him on Friday. I felt His presence beside me. I sobbed out my gratitude for the victory He had gained here. I needed that kind of victory too. I prayed that God would keep me faithful and give me the courage to share the gospel with everyone no matter what the future held.

I don't know how long I stayed on my knees pouring out love and appreciation to Jesus; but the experience was so sacred, so precious, I didn't want it to end. The hour grew late, and we returned to our hotel. A few days later we were back in Lebanon. My experience in the Garden of Gethsemane, however, would stay with me for the rest of my life. In the next few years I would recall the precious hour I had spent on my knees praying where Jesus himself had prayed, and it would give me strength to face impossible situations. I had fallen deeply in love with Jesus, and nothing could ever separate me from His love.

CHAPTER 8

TO MOVE OR NOT TO MOVE; THAT WAS THE QUESTION

Everyone in the mountains, except us, seemed to be moving somewhere. The summer holidays were over, and the vacationers were returning to their coastal homes in Lebanon or traveling back to their countries—Arabia, Kuwait, Iraq, Jordan, etc. Lebanon, the Switzerland of the Middle East, had hummed with tourists all summer, but now that autumn had arrived, there was an emptiness in the mountains. We felt a special void after Michael, Yusif, and the Swaidans left Beit Meri for Middle East College.

Our summer had been somewhat disappointing to us—we could not point to a single soul saved as a result of our work. A small consolation was the knowledge that we had planted the seeds of truth in the hearts of many people from other Arab countries who vacationed in Beit Meri that summer. But being young and impatient, we wanted to see the results here and now—not 20 years down the road.

There was, of course, the providential meeting with Edmond Shammas, but we did not know if that would ever be beneficial to God's work—especially if we didn't move to North Lebanon. We were happy that Edmond had decided to attend MEC instead of going to the states. We hoped that he would become an Adventist at the college; this possibility gave us some satisfaction.

MIDGE IN LEBANON

Then too, there were the Haddad children who seemed quite attracted to Adventism, but that was not necessarily a result of our effort. There were other influences that had already been at work in their lives. First and foremost, their mother was already a baptized member. Our effort was the second time for them to hear the doctrines. The previous winter the Haddads had customarily attended the afternoon youth meetings held in the hotel's dining room by the college students. When Anees couldn't walk because of his injuries from the bus accident, college students carried him to the programs. The loving care of MEC youth made a lasting impression upon Anees, Mary, and Edmond. Therefore, we hoped that the Haddad youth would accept all the Bible truths.

In the meantime, the question of what the mission would do with the Olsons was of vital interest to Wayne and me. First, they voted to move us to the college where Wayne would be dean of men, and I would teach the missionaries' children. Before we made that move, however, plans changed again. This time they voted for us to move to Istanbul, Turkey, where Wayne would take charge of the mission. To us, this plan seemed contrary to the will of God, but we left the decision to the committee. Wayne asked the mission to send him to Turkey by train to look over the situation. Then he would know more about the church, the country, and which of our possessions we should take with us to Turkey.

As I went to the double doors of our apartment to kiss Wayne goodbye, a dream I had in college four years earlier flashed into my mind. (See book 2, chapter 9 of the Midge series). Back then I had dreamed that I stood at double doors like these, kissing my husband, a man with black hair and brown eyes, while I held a year-old baby girl in my arms. The exact duplication of that dream at this moment, sent shivers through me.

TO MOVE OR NOT TO MOVE; THAT WAS THE QUESTION

"I have seen this scenario before in a dream, Wayne," I said solemnly. "When I asked God to let me know whether I should marry Peter or not, this is the exact scene I had in my dream—I was kissing you goodbye as we stood in these double doors, and Ronnie was the baby girl I held. It just seems too awesome to be real. Now I am convinced that God planned for us to get married and work in the Middle East. I hope I'm not putting too much significance in a dream."

"Well, did your dream mean we should move to Turkey?" Wayne asked.

"I don't know about that," I answered. "I only saw this scene—telling you goodbye. Whatever that means, and maybe it doesn't mean anything. I have no impressions about Turkey."

"I've sort of set my heart on going to Turkey now," Wayne admitted. "Of course, what little Arabic we know won't do us any good there. Well, take good care of yourselves while I'm gone." Wayne planted another quick kiss on each of us and raced down the steps to his waiting taxi.

Mary Nassimian stayed with me in Beit Meri while Wayne was gone. There was no one living in the first two floors of our apartment building, nor the hotels, nor most of the other buildings in the town, either. The emptiness of everything gave the village the eerie feeling of a ghost town. Mary and I walked Ronnalee outside every day, but at night we holed up in the apartment with the shutters and doors locked. Someone had told us that criminals often escaped to the mountain villages during the winter and hid out from the law in empty buildings. I didn't know if this was true, but I was gullible enough to believe it was possible. However, people like the Haddads who lived in the mountain village the year around never mentioned having any encounters with criminals. So the skeptic part of me enabled me to sleep well every night.

The first Friday Wayne was gone Mary and I made preparations to attend a big rally in Beirut the next day. After doing the Friday's work we took our showers, ate supper, and put Ronnie to bed. Then we locked the doors, put on our robes, and settled into our favorite easy chairs to read stories from the YOUTH'S INSTRUCTOR. About 8 p.m. I thought I heard Mary say, "Go to the Haddad house."

"Are you crazy, Mary?" I asked her. "You know I'm a born coward. I'd never go to the Haddad house on a dark, cold night like this."

"Ah, what are you talking about, Mrs. Olson?" Mary asked innocently.

"Well, you just told me to go to Haddads' house, didn't you?"

Mary looked mystified. "I haven't said anything, and I certainly would not suggest that you go to the Haddad house tonight!"

"I guess it was just my imagination," I replied, slightly embarrassed.

Five minutes later I seemed to hear the same thing—"GO TO THE HADDAD HOME." Quickly I looked up from my paper at Mary. I detected nothing in her demeanor to indicate that she had said anything. She was deeply engrossed in her reading, so I said nothing to her and tried to continue reading my story. The third time I heard the same instructions, I could stand it no longer. I arose, dressed, and grabbed my coat and scarf.

"Mary, I'm going to the Haddads. I don't know why I feel impressed to visit them tonight, but I know I must. I

TO MOVE OR NOT TO MOVE; THAT WAS THE QUESTION

can't get rid of this feeling. Three times I have heard, or thought I heard, someone say, 'Go to the Haddads.'"

Mary sat bolt upright. "But aren't you afraid?" she asked, almost in awe.

"Scared to death," I admitted honestly. "Just pray for me."

As I walked the quarter mile through the deserted streets to Haddads' house, I shivered in the cold wind and jumped at every rattle of a shutter slamming or a dog barking. When I walked up the steps and knocked at Haddads' door, Victoria welcomed me.

"Come on in, my sister," she said smiling. "I've just been lying here praying that you would come tonight." She pointed at the children who were gathered around a table studying their school lessons for Saturday's classes.

I knew immediately that her concern was for her children who felt they must attend their high school in Brommana on Saturdays. (All schools in Lebanon meet for half-day instructions on Saturdays.) Mrs. Haddad, being a new Adventist, didn't know what to advise her children. Absenting themselves from Saturday classes would surely bring repercussions on them.

Victoria, who had not been feeling well that day, laid back down on the couch and called me to her side. She talked quietly, "I don't want them to go to school on Sabbath—especially since they are convinced that it is God's holy day. I don't think they should study school lessons on Friday nights, either."

I shook my head, breathed a prayer, and walked over to the table where the children were sitting. I chit-chatted a bit with the kids. I knew them well and loved them. We had gone to meetings together, eaten together, and played games together. Now I felt compelled to do some religious counseling with them. I wasn't really that much older than Anees—perhaps eight years—and I hardly felt capable of advising this young man, Mary, and Edmond.

Then thoughts began to formulate in my mind. First I told them the story of Olga, a girl in Eastern Europe, who had serious educational problems because she kept the Sabbath. (Was it providential that I had just read this story before leaving my apartment for Haddads' house?) Olga had completed her medical course with flying colors; she only needed to take the state examinations to be certified to practice her profession. Olga prayed that God would intervene on her behalf, but the exam was given on Saturday anyway. She didn't take the test and, therefore, didn't get certified. She studied some more medicine and waited to take the exam the next year. Again the test was given on Saturday. The third year arrived and once again the exam was scheduled for Saturday. Without certification Olga could not practice medicine anywhere. Were her years of medical education to be wasted? No! The third year the test was re-scheduled for Thursday. This time Olga took the test, rated highest among the examinees, was certified, and placed as a doctor in the best state facility. Her faith had been rewarded.

Now I broached the subject for which I had unwittingly gone to the Haddads' home. I know it isn't easy to go to non-Adventist schools and keep the Sabbath. I went to a public school and, although I never had to go to school on Saturdays, I was urged to participate in sports, music programs, and speaking contests that took place on Saturdays. I lost my chance to win the district speaking contest because I would not perform on Sabbath. Although the principal was upset with me, I knew that contests, music festivals and all other secular activities should be set aside on Sabbath.

TO MOVE OR NOT TO MOVE; THAT WAS THE QUESTION

I think you believe in the sacredness of the Sabbath and all of the other tenets of faith as taught by the Seventh-day Adventist Church. We are hoping you young people will join your mother in keeping all of the truths taught in the Bible. With your talents, I know God has plans for you."

I said more, and they asked questions. At last there was nothing more to say. Either the Haddad children would make their decision to keep the Sabbath holy or not. I felt it was absolutely vital that they take a stand now, tonight, at the beginning of the school year. Delay would only cause more problems later. The atmosphere was charged with emotion as I watched these youth struggle to make their decision. Finally, I suggested that we kneel in prayer. As I prayed I could hear Victoria over on the couch whispering amens.

When we arose from our knees, I talked directly to Anees. "Do you remember the story of Daniel? He was only a year older than you when he took his stand to remain true to God. Are you courageous enough to be a Daniel?"

Anees looked me in the eye, put out his hand and said, "By the grace of God, I am. I will keep the Sabbath and all of God's truths."

Then I turned to Mary. "Remember Queen Esther? She too made a brave decision. She was willing to perish, if need be, to save her people and uphold faith in God."

Tears glistened in Mary's eyes as she closed her school books and piled them on the table, indicating that she had made her decision.

Then I turned to Edmond. He was a happy-go-lucky, 13-year-old that seemed to be more mischievous than serious. "Edmond, will you follow the example of your brother and sister?"

Edmond nodded. Over on the couch Mrs. Haddad was wiping tears from her eyes. I could actually feel the presence of the Holy Spirit in the room. I was thrilled with the faith of these brave young people. I knew the angels were rejoicing with me, but probably were not as choked up as I was. I turned and hugged Mary and Victoria and squeezed the hands of Anees and Edmond.

"God bless you," I managed to say. "And, by the way, there is a full day of meetings scheduled down at the Mouseitbe Church tomorrow. Would you kids like to go down there with Mary, Ronnie, and me? We could stop by and pick you up about 8:45."

"Sure, we'd love to go," they all agreed. Mrs. Haddad declined, as I knew she would—she got deathly car sick—but she was happy for the children to go.

Everyone at Mouseitbe was happy to learn that the Haddad children had taken their stand for Jesus. Later that fall, Pastor Chafic Srour baptized Anees, Mary, and Edmond in the Mediterranean Sea.

That winter the three Haddad children were constantly hassled by their teachers for missing Saturday's classes. Anees was the special target of the principal. At the close of the school year, the final examinations were given on Saturday, and the Haddad children missed them. In spite of the fact that all three youth ranked highest in their classes on their daily school work, the principal failed them in several classes. Furthermore, he sent a letter home with Anees which stated that he would not be admitted to school the following year unless he promised to attend Saturday classes.

TO MOVE OR NOT TO MOVE; THAT WAS THE QUESTION

The next school year God opened a way for the Haddad family to move onto the campus of MEC. There the children completed their college education and all three did become important workers in the SDA church work. (See appendix)

A few days after my night visit to Haddads, a letter arrived from Wayne. He was excited with the prospects of moving to Turkey. "You might as well sell the kerosene stove," he suggested. "They cook with butane here."

That sounded great to me. Although my kerosene cook stove was better than most, it was bothersome to light, cooked food more slowly, and had a smell that I didn't like. So I sold my stove and a few other items that Wayne thought we would not need in Turkey. I started packing, but I felt ambivalent about the move. In one way, I was excited about going to Turkey and getting settled permanently; on the other hand, I felt we would be running away from the mission God had selected for us. I assuaged my conscience by letting the mission committee take the responsibility for moving us wherever they felt best.

A week later Wayne arrived home.

"Well, when do we move?" I asked him trying to suppress the excitement that had been building within me the last few days.

"I'm not sure," Wayne answered slowly, a furrow crossing his brow.

"WHAT?" I exploded. "What do you mean? What's happened now?"

"Well, the folks in Turkey are already doing a good job. Aram Ashod, the current mission president, speaks six languages fluently—Armenian, Greek, and Turkish among them. Mr. Barlas, the colporteur, is doing a

MIDGE IN LEBANON

terrific job. The Bible worker, Miss Yabraxie, definitely knows what she is doing. I just don't see the need to send two young upstarts like us up there for a church of only 65 members. What can we do that the workers there now aren't already doing?"

"I'm sure I don't know," I answered, somewhat disappointed with this report. "If they don't send us to Turkey, where will they move us?"

My question was the same as that still on the mission committee's agenda. Wayne appeared before the committee as requested and expressed his concern to them about Turkey needing our services.

In the meantime, Elder George Keough returned to Lebanon and met with the mission committee. He was a man of action and, as he told us the story, he said something like this:

"Brethren, I see absolutely no sense in sending the Olsons to Turkey. I spent a year teaching them Arabic and orienting them to the Arab Lands—not Turkey. I understand that this summer they began to get a grasp of Arabic and fit right in with the people. We bring missionaries out here to teach at the college or to head up mission departments. Why aren't we bringing out missionaries to preach the gospel to the people? The Olsons came here with the express call and purpose of doing pioneer mission work in North Lebanon. Unless we send evangelists out there on the firing line, the gospel will never get beyond the Beirut area. The trouble in Tripoli has subsided. I believe the Olsons will go and should go there. It's a risk we and they will have to take. I move that the Olsons be sent to Tripoli, North Lebanon, immediately."

Keough's speech must have been convincing. The matter of what to do with the Olsons was settled. The committee voted unanimously to move us to Tripoli. We

TO MOVE OR NOT TO MOVE; THAT WAS THE QUESTION

were satisfied with this decision. God had worked out His plan for us.

Now I wished I hadn't sold my kerosene cook stove.

CHAPTER 9

TO THE SHORES OF TRIPOLI

"Tripoli! The U.S. Marines sing about it. You know—'From the Halls of Montezuma to the Shores of Tripoli,'" I sang.

"No, that's Tripoli, North Africa," Wayne interrupted.

"I know that. But since North Lebanon's Tripoli is on the shores of the Mediterranean Sea, I'll modify the song: 'From the plains of South Dakota to the shores of Tripoli,'" I sang lustily.

Wayne grinned and patted my shoulder. "Midge, you'll never make Broadway."

I knew that too.

"Seriously, how do we go about pioneering Adventist work in Tripoli?" Wayne questioned.

"I don't know, but I do know one person from North Lebanon—Edmond Shammas. Remember?"

Of course Wayne remembered Edmond Shammas from Shekka. We had spent a day and a half with him in Beit Meri in concentrated Bible study. Since then, Edmond had canceled his plans to go to the States for his college education and enrolled in MEC instead. Edmond had become a very special person to us.

"Speaking of Edmond, let's go down to MEC right now and discuss with him our move into his territory," Wayne suggested. In moments we were off for the college.

MIDGE IN LEBANON

"Guess what, Edmond?" I began. "The mission has voted for us to move to Tripoli, and we need your advice. What should we know about Tripoli, and how do we go about finding housing there? We've never even been there..."

"Oh, no problem!" Edmond interjected enthusiastically. "I know Tripoli well. I attended the Presbyterian Boys School there. I'll take a few days off from school and acquaint you with the town and some of my friends. I want you to meet my family too. And, aaah, will you give them Bible studies?"

"Of course," Wayne promised. "We came to Lebanon to do just that—study the Bible with any interested soul."

The next morning Edmond, Wayne, Ronnie, and I drove the 50 miles north to Tripoli. On the way we stopped in Shekka where Edmond introduced us to his family. They were very friendly, cultured people and invited us to stop at their house for dinner on our way back to Beirut.

In Tripoli, Edmond took us to see the manager of a big city bank where his father did business. After the introductions were over, Fuad Melham and Edmond conversed in Arabic. We supposed they were discussing housing for us.

Then turning to us, Fuad shocked us by speaking in the best of the King's English. "I would suggest," he said, "that you take an apartment in the newer part of the Christian sector of the city. In fact, I remember seeing a duplex in that area that has recently been completed. It may not be rented yet. Let's go over there right now. We might catch the owner at home for lunch."

We acted upon Fuad's suggestion immediately and drove to the pie-shaped piece of land with streets running on all three sides. The duplex filled the front side of a main street. A shared portico had pillars and glazed-tile flooring which made an impressive entrance. The other two sides of the property were bordered by a six-foot wall just perfect for containing my toddler if I could teach her not to destroy the flowers and young trees. The set-up was ideal for our needs, but could we afford it?

While we waited for the owner to come home for lunch, Wayne explained to Fuad that, although we were Americans, we were missionaries and, therefore, not monied people. Wayne stated the maximum rent that the mission had authorized us to pay for housing. Fuad gave a low whistle. "That's not much for housing in Tripoli, but we'll see what we can do."

When the owner came, he gave us a tour of the empty duplex—three spacious bedrooms, living room, family room, dining room, and baths. The only skimpy room was the kitchen. We wanted this place but....

The owner quoted a high rental price. We prayed silently while Fuad countered with an offer much less than our maximum allowance. We were embarrassed, yet fascinated by the bargaining process. Fuad pointed out that we were clean people and had only one SMALL child. More discussion ensued while we prayed some more. Finally, Fuad cinched the deal by promising the owner that we would pay six months rent cash in advance. We signed the contract for a year's lease with only the verbal agreement that we would bring the money the next week. What amazed us was that the owner handed over the key, trusting us to keep our promise! I liked doing business with a Lebanese. It was just like dealing with an honest Midwesterner from my childhood days in South Dakota.

Edmond spent the afternoon taking us around Tripoli and introducing us to his friends. He gave them our address and told them to visit us in a week. Then we returned to Shekka and dined with Edmond's family. We discovered that Mr. Shammas was comfortably wealthy. He owned the garage, service station, and other properties in Shekka. The Shammas family treated us royally; they even extended a permanent invitation for us to dine with them every Thursday evening and to hold Bible studies in their home. What a marvelous opening for us!

We returned to Beirut and dropped Edmond off at the college. Then we shared our news with our mentor, George Keough, who wished us God's blessings. The next week the college truck moved our belongings to Tripoli. We took along all of the evangelistic equipment and stored it in a bedroom. The pump organ, however, we placed in our living room.

The first Friday night, some of Edmond's high school friends came to visit—Clement, George, Adul, and Zaher. When they saw the organ, they hinted that they would enjoy singing some of the Christian hymns they had learned at the Presbyterian Boys School. So I played while they sang—sometimes in English and sometimes in Arabic. Then, while we got better acquainted, I served them cookies and punch.

"That was a nice way to begin our first Sabbath in North Lebanon," Wayne commented after the boys left.

I concurred. But the next day was the longest and loneliest Sabbath of my whole life. Wayne, Ronnie, and I were the only Seventh-day in Tripoli, a city of 100,000 people. We studied the Sabbath School lesson together, but we had done that all week. We read, but Ronnie got bored with that.

Late in the afternoon we drove a mile to the seashore. We fed bread to the sea gulls and watched the fishermen cast off for their evening of fishing in the open seas. Then

TO THE SHORES OF TRIPOLI

we watched the last pink and gold fade from the western sky as the sun sank into the sea—from the shores of Tripoli.

CHAPTER 10

STARTS AND STOPS

We had barely gotten started with Bible studies in Tripoli when political conditions brought things to an abrupt halt. It happened, fortunately, during a visit from Chafic Srour, one of the national pastors. Wayne and Chafic weren't expecting any trouble the day they drove into the city "just to have a look around", but they found it, anyway. They first noticed an excited crowd gathered in the City Square, so they went over to investigate the reason.

"Let's get out of here, quick!" Chafic whispered to Wayne after he had listened to a few animated speeches.

"Why?" Wayne asked as Chafic pushed him towards his parked car.

"Because your life is in danger! Let's go!" On the way home Chafic explained the situation to Wayne. "The United Nations is threatening to divide Palestine, giving the productive western half to the Jews and the eastern drier region to the Arabs. The Arabs know they are getting the short end of the stick and are angry. They feel it isn't fair for the United Nations to take their country, or any other country, and fill it with European refugees. Why shouldn't every nation be asked to absorb some of them? Naturally the Jews want to go to Palestine, but the Arabs have had much of that land in their possession for centuries—probably since the Babylonian captivity."

MIDGE IN LEBANON

When the men got home, Chafic advised us not to appear in public. Resentment against America and England, who had sponsored the idea of partitioning Palestine, was running very high. Chafic tried to devise a plan to spirit us out of Tripoli and get us to a safer place.

Wayne objected. "We're staying right here. We have faith that God will protect us. Besides, we are American citizens."

"Ho, ho," Chafic laughed satirically. "Americans are mortal too, and bullets don't have favorite nationalities. Be realistic!"

One Middle East missionary, the Apostle Paul, advised us to be wise. He used his best judgment and left Ephesus when political turmoil threatened to end his career."

Chafic had made his point. Since we understood very little Arabic, we really didn't know what was going on. Chafic did. Concerned Christian brother that he was, Chafic went to the store and bought a week's supply of groceries. Then he stayed with us a few days until things simmered down.

Shortly after Chafie left, I thought it would be safe for me to take Ronnie outside for a walk. On the street I met some young Lebanese men who recognized me as an American. They shouted angrily at me and pushed me off the sidewalk. I was thankful when they left. No harm had come to Ronnie or me other than being frightened and roughed up a bit. I hurried home by a circuitous route. Now I knew that Chafic's warning had been justified.

Eventually I learned to appreciate the Arabs' point of view. It seemed to them and us that the big nations and the UN decided their fate without ever understanding the political issues. It reminded me of a city slicker

STARTS AND STOPS

trying to tell the old farmer how to milk his cows. Living with the Lebanese and learning their language was the best way for me to "see things through their eyes." When we finally came to KNOW the Arabs, they became our favorite people in the world.

Things settled down, and we began Bible studies again with Edmond's friends. Early on the morning of November 30, 1947, we were surprised by a hurried visit from Fuad Melhelm, the nice banker. "Don't go out of your house today," he warned looking very grim. "Keep your shutters and doors closed! There is danger out there for you foreigners—especially Americans. Yesterday, November 29, the United Nations actually voted to partition Palestine. This decision will drive a million Palestinian Arabs from their homes. When the British troops withdraw from their current peace-keeping mission, there will be civil war between the Arabs and the Jews. The Arabs have fought on the side of the allies during the two great wars. Now they feel betrayed. When the United States voted at the UN to divide Palestine between the Jews and the Arabs, in reality they voted to give the land, businesses, and homes of the Arabs to the Jews. The people of Tripoli are burning and looting Jewish shops in protest. In their anger, they will not differentiate between an American missionary and a political enemy. Since I can't get you to Beirut right now, please stay in your house until I can. I'll come back this noon to check on you. After dark, I'll smuggle you to our home where you can stay until the situation changes. Mother is worried about your safety. Goodbye for now." And Fuad raced off in his car.

This time we didn't need a lecture on precaution; I remembered my earlier experience of being pushed off the sidewalk. We closed the slatted shutters so it would appear that no one was home. Ronnie settled into playing in the semidarkened house while Wayne and I contemplated the future.

"How are we ever going to preach the gospel in North Lebanon if we have to hole up every few weeks for political disturbances?" Wayne questioned.

I shrugged my shoulders. "I don't know, but I do know that God has already 'opened the Red Sea' for us. Moses had a few conflicts on his way to the promised land, and it looks as if we are having our starts and stops too."

"Yes," Wayne agreed. "We probably shouldn't be overly concerned; God will take care of His work and us."

"When I was younger, Mom tried to teach me patience. 'Wait on the Lord, Midge,' she'd say. Maybe we'll have to do some waiting."

"Right you are—this time," Wayne conceded giving me a little squeeze.

A few weeks after the partitioning of Palestine was voted, our life in Tripoli settled into a routine. We had Thursday night meetings in Shekka and weekend meetings at our house in Tripoli. Sometimes Adventists from Beirut came to spend a few hours with us, brightening the lonely days. They will never know what a lift their visits gave me. Though we kept busy, I missed the social life I had enjoyed in Beit Meri. I had been born into a large family, and I longed to be surrounded by familiar people.

Those lonely days were a trial for me. It would have helped if the mission had hired someone to teach us Arabic. Unfortunately, they did not have the money at this period when we had the time and the incentive to learn it. Being isolated as we were from an English-speaking society, we needed to know Arabic for our own sanity, safety, and work,

STARTS AND STOPS

One day we got a brilliant idea. We persuaded Clement, a friend of Edmond's, to teach us Arabic three nights per week and paid him a nominal fee from our meager salary. But Clement was more interested in improving his English, so we learned very little Arabic from him. So much for that brilliant idea. Since not knowing Arabic limited us in our work, we prayed that God would give us the gift of tongues—specifying the Arabic language, of course.

The boys that came to our Bible studies in Tripoli knew English quite well, but we needed a translator for our cottage meetings in Shekka where they understood only Arabic and French. Since we knew neither, we asked Clement to be our translator. There were two drawbacks with this choice: 1) Clement didn't have an adequate vocabulary of religious terms to translate Bible texts accurately; 2) Clement was almost a chain smoker. It didn't quite seem right for a smoker to be translating the Adventist message when our church stressed health principles. Furthermore, Clement scared me silly as I watched him turn the pages of our only Arabic Bible with a lit cigarette in his hand. I was afraid he would catch the Word on fire. Beside all of that, tobacco smoke added to my nausea—I was pregnant.

When we went to Beirut for our monthly pay check, we discussed this problem with Elder George Keough. "Say, would you like for me to go up to Shekka and help you out?" he asked, grinning like a boy waiting to be invited to stick his hand in the cookie jar. He couldn't conceal his excitement at the prospects of getting into evangelism.

"Yes, we would," Wayne assured Keough.

From then on, Elder Keough came up to Shekka as often as he could get transportation. He delighted the people with his knowledge of Arabic and the Bible. When the Elder couldn't come, we still had to use the chain-smoking Clement. The studies were moving along without further starts and stops, but it was obvious that we needed a permanent, Seventh-day Adventist translator to work with us. The mission agreed to send a college student as soon as school was over. We were thankful that, at last, help was on the way.

CHAPTER 11

A WELL IS A HOLE IN THE GROUND

In March, the mission gave Wayne an additional assignment—drill for water at MEC. They knew that the spring on the college property would never supply their needs. Even after the heavy winter rains the spring never increased its volume sufficiently to half fill the reservoirs. Since Wayne knew a little about drilling wells, his help was enlisted. March 7 Wayne made a model well drilling rig. Then he, Stanley Johnson, and the industrial arts students put the real thing together. They started drilling two weeks later.

We spent most of the next three months at the college, going home only for the Thursday night meetings in Shekka and the weekend meetings at our house in Tripoli. Edmond Shammas often went home with us Thursday after classes and translated for the evening meetings at his home. This was a blessing because it saved us from using Clement.

We enjoyed our work weeks at the college. Sometimes I gave readings for the college programs, and Wayne led out in student games. We stayed with the Moles at the Villa, a palatial home which the college rented to house four faculty families. Since I was still very ill with my pregnancy, I was relieved to have Ronnalee in the tender, efficient care of Jeannette Mole.

Wayne spent all of the daylight hours up on the college hill with his rig. Everyone watched anxiously as the bit dug deeper into the ground. At times, a trickle of water filtered into the hole—enough to stir our hopes. But the well could always be pumped dry in a few minutes. Wayne had to keep drilling deeper.

April moved into May and still no significant amount of water was found. Soon Wayne would have to quit drilling for water because our effort in Shekka would begin in July. The mission was sending Michael Kebbas and Moses Ghazal to help us during the months of July, August, and September. Wayne prayed that the hole he was drilling would result in a geyser of water by mid-June. He wanted time to get ready for our first effort in North Lebanon. Although a good well was very important to the college, evangelism was more important to us.

One day when Arthur Keough, educational secretary for the union, was on the drill site, he surprised Wayne with a suggestion. "Why don't you take a respite from this well business and go on a vacation down to Egypt?"

"That sounds great, but, aah, I don't know if I have the time. Why?" Wayne grunted as he pulled more dirt up from the hole.

"Well, I'm going down there the last part of May to inspect the schools and visit the churches with Neal Wilson, president of the Egyptian mission," he answered in his tactful, unhurried manner. With Arthur, you knew there was a motive behind this Englishman's speech. Wayne waited for the disclosure. "We will be visiting the villages of upper Egypt where my father pioneered the work 40 years ago, much as you are doing now in North Lebanon. I thought it would be encouraging for you to see the results of father's small beginnings.

We left the drilling to Mr. Johnson and the boys and flew to Egypt on May 19, 1948. Our visit to upper Egypt with Arthur and Neal inspired us greatly. Although the life of the villagers in southern Egypt is harsh and demanding, the Adventists were a happy, friendly, and devoted people. Their adobe huts scarcely protected them from the sun's scorching heat, and they enjoyed few of the amenities of the Lebanese. Although the Nile River is the source of life in Egypt because it provides all the water to irrigate their three yearly crops, it also supplies a variety of organisms and parasites in their drinking cups. This decreases their life expectancy by many years. Therefore, Neal bought bottled pop to drink and insisted that we eat only hot, cooked food.

We visited many churches in Upper Egypt. Ronnie and I sat on mats on the women's side. Through the faded curtain that separated us, I saw the men sitting on backless benches, and I envied them that luxury. I wanted to join Wayne, but custom would not allow it. Because of my limited Arabic vocabulary, I had to converse with the women mainly through signs and wonders. They could see I was pregnant and they wished for me the greatest of all blessings—that the baby was a son. In the Arab world, a son is special because he cares for his parents in their old age. During the worship service, they petitioned God to bless Neal and Eleanor, who were childless at this time, with a son. Less than two years later God gave Wilsons a son they named Teddy.

I was impressed by the way Neal and Arthur conversed freely with the people in Arabic. I prayed the day would soon come when I could do that too.

We were thrilled to see the progress of the work in the villages of upper Egypt, and we expressed this to Arthur. He smiled, satisfied that his scheme had succeeded. "Now you see how father's pioneer mission work has turned out. I believe that, for you, digging for souls will be more rewarding and permanent than digging a well. Think about getting back to your original assignment. Don't feel obligated to fulfill all the requests our well-meaning brethren lay upon you. Soul winning in new areas demands more than full-time work, or else interest fades and the results are small. Sort of like the well at the college—a deep hole but only a trickle." The object lesson was not lost on us.

After the work week was over, Neal took us down to Luxor. The restored remains of this ancient, once-grandiose city of the proud pharaohs overwhelmed us. It was built over a period of hundreds of years when Egypt dominated the world. These huge structures and the fantastic art work was all done by the slave labor of the Hebrews, Syrians, Canaanites, and other subjugated people. It was here that Queen Hatshepsut drew her foster child, Moses, from the sacred Nile.

I stepped back in time 3,500 years. In my imagination I pictured teen-age Moses running down the paved street to the landing dock on the Nile. Like the rest of the boys, he climbed upon the lime-stone animals that lined the avenue and watched the boats plying their way along the Nile River. Even though the late May temperature soared above 120 degrees, two-year old Ronnalee attempted to climb upon those same stone creatures that must have fascinated young Moses and the Egyptian children. Moses, like us, must have been staggered at the immensity and beauty of the temple built to honor the sun god, Ra.

We crossed the Nile on a faluka (small sail boat). I wondered how many times Moses had crossed with the funeral barge to the "city of the dead", the hillocks where the pharaohs had their tombs carved into the rock. Moses studied science, medicine, astronomy, warfare, etc. in the school for palace royalty. I suppose he must have learned to write hieroglyphics too. The plastered walls of the tombs are covered with this pictorial form of writing which give an exaggerated, complimentary account of the occupant of that tomb.

We returned to Cairo via the fast, sleeper-coach train.

There we went to the pyramids and sphinx, rode camels, and did the things tourists do in Egypt. On May 31, Gordon Zytkoskee offered to take us to the Abu Ali Mosque, famous for its polished alabaster walls, architectural beauty, and verses from the Koran written in artistic Arabic script around its dome. Cairo is a large city (over 14 million today), and the streets are not well marked, so Gordon stopped to ask a policeman directions to the mosque. The policeman immediately left his post directing traffic, got into Gordon's car, and ordered him to drive to the central police station. There we were held in custody all afternoon.

Why? We supposed we were suspected of being Jewish spies. What was worse, none of us had our passports with us for identification. Our passports were at the Lebanese consul getting our return visas stamped in them, and Gordon's was at home. We weren't sufficiently fluent in Arabic to exonerate ourselves, either, so we waited for the police chief to return from his siesta.

Two hours passed and I was growing impatient. It was hot and I was hungry, thirsty, pregnant, and tired of running after a two-year old. "Did you ever hear of a Jew named OLSON?" I asked the policeman a bit sarcastically. "Besides, why would a Jew want to go to the mosque?"

"Boom, BOOM, maybe," he answered in his limited English indicating that we might want to blow up the place. Through squinted eyes he pointed at Gordon, "Him name—no good."

MIDGE IN LEBANON

"I hadn't thought of it before but ZYTKOSKEE is sort of a dangerous sounding name. Is it Korean, Irish, Danish, or none of the above?" I teased Gordon.

Gordon wasn't talking anymore. The heat and the incredulity of the situation had sapped him.

Little Ronnie was a pretty good sport. She chased flies and stomped on her shadow while we withered in the heat. She finally won their sympathy, so the policemen gave her some popcorn and soda pop. Not the best lunch for a toddler, but Ronnie gobbled it up faster than the food I usually fed her.

Finally, about 5 p.m., the chief came and immediately released us. We had been under arrest for four and a half hours. Now I knew how dangerous it was to associate oneself with a minister by the name of Zytkoskee who asked directions.

All too soon our holiday was over and we had to return to Lebanon. On the flight home, our twin-engine Air Liban plane was attacked by an unidentified fighter plane off the coast of Haifa, Israel. As the pilot nosed our plane for the sea, I saw my life pass before me. My face smashed into the seat in front of me, but I didn't care—it would all be over soon, anyway. I was disturbed in my hurried prayer by the lady behind me who got down on her hands and knees in the aisle and addressed the Virgin Mary. In the process, she slid all the way up to the pilot. But before she could be of any assistance to him, the pilot adjusted the flaps and headed for the stars. We were thrown back into our seats while the woman skidded back down the aisle. When the plane leveled out, the lady crawled back into her seat. She never regained her composure or her color; her nylons were hopelessly tattered and her clothes askew. We were all thankful when our plane landed safely at the Beirut airport the afternoon of June 2.

A WELL IS A HOLE IN THE GROUND

Before going home, we stopped at the college to see the progress made at the well drilling site in our absence—no water yet, just a dry hole. After the weekend, Wayne returned to the college to drill for water, but with less enthusiasm, thanks to Arthur.

June 12 we thrilled with joy as we witnessed the baptism of Edmond Shammas, the first spiritual fruits from North Lebanon.

Excerpts from Wayne's diary for the next few days reads:

June 17—drilling with success.

June 20—MEC graduation. Well is 24 1/2 meters deep.

June 27—Boys got the bit stuck in the well. Can't budge it.

June 28—bit is hopelessly stuck. Must start all over and drill new hole. I can't do it because Michael and Moses come to North Lebanon tomorrow for the summer effort. The well is just a hole in the ground. I hope the gospel work in North Lebanon will have better results—a geyser of souls would be good.

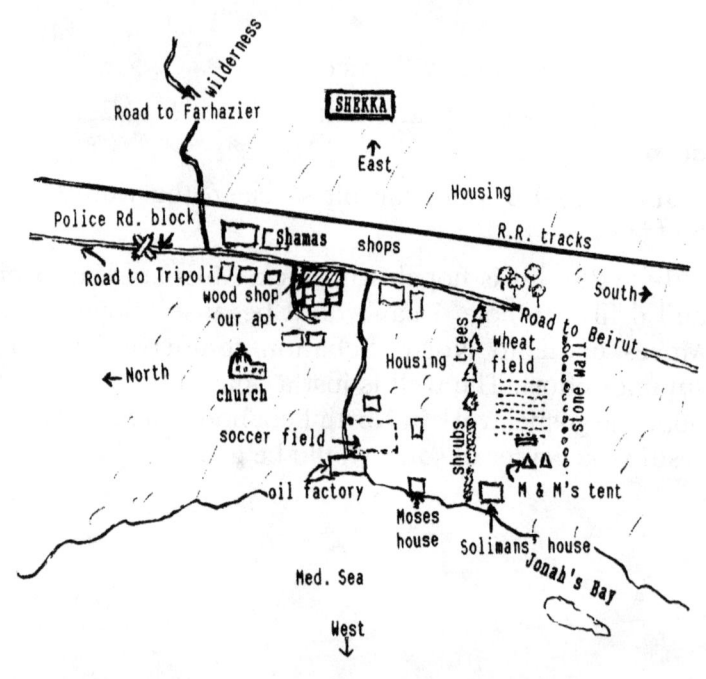

CHAPTER 12

TROUBLE IN THE WHEAT FIELD

The meetings in Tripoli had dwindled to almost nothing, but the group in Shekka continued to grow until the Shammas's dining and living room could no longer contain them. It was difficult for the hospitable Shammas family to turn folks away, but there was no choice. One evening after the meeting we discussed this problem with the most zealous of the group. They and we believed the message should be shared with everyone in the village who wanted to hear it. We had already searched for a larger place that we could rent but found there was simply nothing available.

Suddenly Mrs. Soliman's face lit up. "I've got it," she said triumphantly. "We have just harvested the wheat by our house. If we run sheep in there for a few days, they'll eat down the stubble, leaving it very clean. We can extend electricity to the site from our house, and you can set up chairs and a platform. There will be plenty of room for everyone in our wheat field, and the access is easy—right off the main road. It will be an inspiring place with a canopy of stars above and the waves from Jonah's Bay lapping the shore just a stone's throw away to the west. What do you think?"

The idea was so novel that it took us all by surprise. Then everyone agreed that Mrs. Soliman had the ideal solution.

On July 5, Wayne started working on a permit to hold public meetings. Lebanon had religious freedom, but the law required a government permit for any public meetings held outside of a registered church or mosque. This regulation had been overlooked by the city fathers in Beit Meri the summer before because of the influence Middle East College had had upon that community. North Lebanon knew nothing about Adventists; besides, the political climate was different.

In the Middle East, in general, there exists a blending of religion with politics. This situation is accentuated in Lebanon where the country was/is almost equally divided between Moslems and Christians. Tensions had already spilled over into the political arena threatening a civil war. (Which finally broke out between the Moslem and Christian factions in 1975). Therefore, public meetings of any kind without a special permit were forbidden for fear they would be used as an excuse to foment an insurrection. Getting a permit was an absolute must.

We soon discovered, however, that getting a permit was far more complicated than we had imagined. July 6 Wayne petitioned the Surete General, the department for internal security, for a permit to hold public evangelistic meetings. Wayne came home feeling rather confident that the permit would be summarily granted. I was happy with that news, but even more pleased to see Mary Nassimian come with Wayne from Beirut. Mary was our capable Armenian friend from the college who had cared for Ronnie the previous summer during our Beit Meri effort. With Mary in charge of our toddler, I was free to work with Wayne.

Then calamity struck. During this extremely busy time of effort preparations, Ronnalee became seriously ill with malaria. Watching our little darling suffer, and realizing that she could possibly die, drained us emotionally. Ronnie was the light of our lives, God's special blessing, the epitome of everything that reaches the zenith. It was difficult to persuade the two-year-old that she must swallow the bitter, liquid quinine, but without it her fever soared dangerously high. Fortunately, Ronnie had an amiable, good-sport disposition that worked in our favor to gain her cooperation. She would shiver when she saw the spoonful of quinine approach her mouth but would gulp it down and snatch the piece of Swiss chocolate we held in front of her as a reward.

While our hearts were burdened with concern for Ronnie, plans for the effort proceeded on schedule. The bus dropped off Michael, Moses, and the camping equipment on the edge of the wheat field. Wayne went out to help them set up camp—one large tent for the boys to live in, and the other to store the organ and other equipment that might be vulnerable to the elements. Moses painted the sign advertising the meetings for Sunday, Tuesday, and Thursday nights. Wayne and Michael bought 100 cheap chairs to seat the audience. They focused a spotlight on the ten commandments which were painted on two vertical 4x8 plywood sheets nailed to the back of the platform. On either side of the commandments, they fastened another plywood sheet painted a glossy white upon which they could project pictures.

With the chairs arranged in rows and the lights strung, we were ready to begin our meetings. Now all we needed was the permit to hold them. That one little obstacle did not blight our expectations. We believed great victories for God would be won here in the wheat field.

The next few days, Wayne continued to chase after the meeting permit but without success. Sunday, July 18, the day our meetings were to begin, arrived, and still we had no permit. Wayne checked with our friends in Shekka who advised us to go ahead with the meetings, anyway, because they believed the permit was most certainly on its way.

Wayne and I left Ronnie with Mary and drove out to Shekka for our opening night. We were as excited as two kids on their first excursion to Disneyland. As we entered the city we noticed a police road block. "Hm, I wonder what kind of criminal they're looking for," I remarked casually.

"Don't know," Wayne answered, "but it must be a big one judging by the number of police."

We watched as they waved car after car through. Wayne rolled down his window as we reached the check-point. The officer scrutinized us carefully. "Here he is! I've got the Americani!" he yelled exultantly to the others.

STUNNED! A microbial word incapable of describing our dismay.

"You must be mistaken," Wayne said catching his breath. "I've done nothing wrong."

"Weren't you going to have a meeting without a permit?"

"Yes, but I have applied for one, and it's only a matter of time until the permit arrives," Wayne explained. "I was told it would be alright for us to begin tonight without it."

"You have that in writing?" the officer questioned.

"Well, no," Wayne admitted. "But what I'll say tonight is non-political. It's just a Bible lecture. Come down to the wheat Field and hear for yourself."

TROUBLE IN THE WHEAT FIELD

"I will escort you down to the wheat field, but I will not permit you to speak except to tell the people there will be no meeting tonight."

As the two policemen climbed into the back seat of our Ford, I whispered to Wayne in English, "I guess you're the 'big one' they were after. Look, I'm tired of being arrested with you—remember Egypt?"

"That wasn't my fault, either, Midge, and you're not funny."

"I know," I sighed, "but it's my way of coping."

We were still aghast when we parked our car on the edge of the wheat field. Moses and Michael, along with our Shekka friends, rushed joyously out to meet us. They stopped short when they saw police step out of our car. Almost immediately, our friends suspected the reason for the police presence and became angry.

"Get off my property, you vermin," Mr. Soliman shouted to the police. "Leave these people alone. I have invited Mr. Olson here to speak to us, and anyone who wants to walk onto my property to hear him is welcome."

"But, it's against the law to hold public meetings without a permit, and we have orders to stop him," the officer snapped. "You are in contempt of the law. I ought to arrest you too."

Things were heating up pretty fast, and the crowd of 50 had already doubled in size. Michael and Moses were trying to defuse the explosive situation.

"I demand to know who's behind these orders to stop the meetings," Afeef yelled above the noise of the crowd. "The priest and a few of his followers, I'd wager."

The police did not take kindly to the nasty remarks being made about them by the crowd, but they were fearfully outnumbered, so they kept their cool. We kept quiet because we did not want to spark any worse trouble. We knew that if the crowd caused a riot, we would be deported from Lebanon.

Finally the police agreed to go with Wayne and Afeef to Batroun, the county seat, to see if the khaimakam (the equivalent of a county sheriff) would issue a temporary permit. As the four drove off, I breathed a sigh of relief and a prayer for their success.

Michael attempted to bring order out of chaos by asking the crowd to be seated. Moses handed out song sheets, I sat down at the organ, and we began the song service. I opened the bellows on the organ, and Moses sang as loudly as possible. Even then, he could not be heard above the crowd. The people were having a great time singing lustily any song they chose from the song sheet to any tune that struck their fancy. The discordance would have sent any musician into outer space. Poor Moses! He looked as if he was about to take off.

The crowd swelled to 250 and then gradually dwindled down to 150. They waited restlessly for Wayne and Afeef to return. As the minutes ticked by, Moses sang himself hoarse while Michael moved cautiously among the crowd trying to maintain order.

Meanwhile, Wayne and Afeef were frantically hunting for the khaimakam's house in Batroun. They finally found it and were greeted warmly by the gentleman. They apologized for disturbing him on a Sunday night and explained the reason for their call. He understood their urgency and graciously wrote the necessary, temporary permit. Then Wayne and Afeef raced back to the wheat field, well over an hour later than when the meeting was scheduled to begin.

By that time, Moses, Michael, and I were emotionally drained by trying to entertain the crowd. Almost 150 people remained, waiting impatiently for Wayne's return. They cheered as Wayne made his way to the platform. Mounting the platform was quite another matter. Since all of the chairs were occupied, 15 young men sat on the platform filling every inch of space. They congenially scrunched together so Wayne could work his way among them. When Wayne finally reached the podium and started to speak, several youth arose and stood behind him. This was a bit disconcerting because, knowing the opposition that existed, Wayne wasn't comfortable with their close proximity.

Then, looking over his shoulder, they read aloud from his typewritten notes. Since they could read the outline much faster than Wayne could elaborate on his topic, they got bored and resorted to reading aloud from the English Bible. This was frustrating to Wayne and agonizing to Moses, our translator, who tried to raise his hoarse voice above the readers' murmurs. It was complete bedlam to us, but the audience enjoyed themselves immensely and promised to return on Tuesday night.

The next day, Wayne and the boys invited the village cleric to the tent and had a two-hour talk with him. It was obvious that the priest had instigated the trouble with the permit. He indicated that he would continue to oppose and persecute us even if he had to take "drastic steps" to remove us. How drastic was "drastic" we wondered, as we assured the priest that we would stay. Of course, we understood the priest's point of view—he was trying to protect his flock against us Protestant foreigners. But he needn't have worried about that—those who usually came to our meetings were the ones who were not loyal members of his church, anyway.

Wayne spent the rest of Monday in Batroun, Shekka, and Amuin; then Batroun and Shekka again, and Tripoli contacting government officials for the permanent permit. Tuesday was also spent seeking a permit. We did have a good meeting on Tuesday night with over 200 in attendance. On Wednesday, however, the Surete General in Tripoli asked us to hold up on the meetings until he could work things out. So Thursday night's meeting was cancelled.

We were thankful when Sabbath came; it had been a long, stressful week. The next week Wayne, Michael, and Moses spent as much time as possible visiting the people who were the most interested. A great deal of Wayne's time, however, was still spent working on the permit. He usually touched base with half a dozen officials several times a week.

On Thursday, July 29, the local authorities issued a bonified temporary permit to Wayne. That night we had a very quiet meeting. People had adjusted to having a religious service in an open field. They sang as best they could the songs that Moses chose. Many, however, still tended to chant in a minor key, but their sensitive ears helped them learn to sing hymns in the major key. No one read Wayne's notes aloud or stood on the platform. Two hundred people heard the message of Daniel 2 on Thursday night. Sunday and Tuesday nights, August 1 and 3, about 150 people were still attending the meetings. Great things were beginning to happen in the wheat field. Our fondest hopes were coming to fruition. Our spirits were soaring somewhere near cloud nine as we reported the amazing turnout to the mission people in Beirut. They too were excited because 150 non-Adventists attending an evangelistic meeting regularly was some kind of record for the Middle East.

Then it happened! Wayne went to the Surete in Tripoli on Thursday, August 5 to pick up his identity card. The official looked very solemn as he broke the bad news.

TROUBLE IN THE WHEAT FIELD

"Mr. Olson, you absolutely must NOT have anymore meetings in Shekka. The bishop* has informed me that you are dividing the village. You must stop!"

"No. Not now," Wayne argued. "Not when things are going so well. Sir, do you know that over 150 people are coming to the meetings because they enjoy studying the Bible? Should they be deprived of this priv…"

"Mr. Olson, please heed my warning," he advised. "There is serious trouble waiting to explode out there in the wheat field in Shekka. Go out there today, now, and spread the word that the meetings are cancelled. Perhaps permanently."

I could tell by the drawn look on Wayne's face as he entered the door that something serious was wrong. His voice trembled as he delivered the regrettable news. I burst into tears and went into the study to talk to God about this turn of events.

I reminded the Lord that this was His work, and many people wanted to hear His word. I asked, perhaps even demanded, that He influence the authorities to reverse the decision. I even questioned why He hadn't figured that out. I had. I cried angry tears and prayed tenaciously. I wouldn't give up. I wanted Him to grant me a positive response like He did for Jacob. But no angel came and wrestled with me, so I gave the Lord a deadline. "I'll wait until 2 o'clock for you to send someone to our house, telling us that we may proceed with the meetings as usual. Where are you, God? You've always been here when we needed you before. Aren't you looking after things in Shekka?"

We waited anxiously, but 2 o'clock came and went. We even gave God an extra hour and nothing happened. Time had run out, so we went out to Shekka and told Michael and Moses that we had to cancel the meetings—orders from the Surete.

The boys were also shaken by this report. None of us could understand why God had allowed this to happen. We prayed together, but our prayers didn't seem to penetrate the tent top. We were quite choked up as Moses took down the sign advertising our meetings. Then Wayne and I returned to Tripoli because the Surete had warned Wayne not even to be in Shekka that night.

We spent a most heartbreaking evening at home; nothing could distract us from our desire to be in Shekka. I could hardly force myself to pray to God because I stiff believed He was to blame. I felt He had abandoned us.

After spending a restless night questioning "WHY", we could stay away no longer. We went out to Shekka to check on the boys. The story Michael and Moses told was incredible.

Early the previous evening our friend, Afeef, was pacing along the roadside by the wheat field. He noticed some young boys with papers in their hands huddled together. He took a few papers from them and was shocked to read the poetry that had been composed by some knowing adult denouncing, insulting, and ridiculing the Adventists. He asked the boys what they planned to do with the papers. "Oh," they responded, "when Olson gets up to preach, we're supposed to jump up on the platform and read these aloud."

The opposition orchestrating this plan knew that this repugnant poetry would infuriate our friends. They would try to stop the boys performance. Angry accusations would then develop into a full-blown fracas. Then from behind stone walls, trees, and a corn field, sharp shooters would drill ammunition into the area. If someone (probably Wayne) just "happened" to get shot in the riot, it would be registered as an accident.

TROUBLE IN THE WHEAT FIELD

We were aghast! Shivers rippled through my body as I thought of what might have been if God would have listened to me. I was deeply humbled and shamed. I begged the Lord to forgive my arrogance and obstinacy. I promised I would never again doubt His leading. Had it been providence that took Wayne to the Surete the very day the opposition planned this attack? Had Wayne not happened to go for his identity card, how would the Surete have located us? He didn't know our address. I bowed my head and thanked my omniscient God for saving us all.

But that was not all. Our enemies were baffled by our absence and wondered who had warned us to shut down our meetings that night, thus delivering us from their treacherous hands. They were angry because their plans had been foiled and determined they would still get revenge.**

Michael and Moses were naturally unaware of their plans, so they bedded down in their tent as usual. About midnight Michael awakened suddenly. He felt something was wrong. "Sit up, Moses, NOW!" he whispered hoarsely.

"But why?" Moses questioned rubbing his eyes.

"I don't know. Just SIT UP!" Michael demanded.

As Moses arose from his mattress, a bullet ripped through the tent where his head had been. The bullet hole was positive proof of our enemies' evil intent. I shivered again, awed by this unmistakable miracle of deliverance.

The trouble in the wheat field closed down our public meetings in Shekka but opened many other doors. People in other locales, hearing of our trouble in Shekka, were curious as to why we were worth such violent opposition. They invited us into their areas so they could hear our message and judge for themselves. So the persecution actually worked favorably to spread the gospel. As we stepped by faith through new doors, God put us in contact with people who were waiting for the message. Our courage would have soared if we could only have looked into the future.

*In this book, Bishop and priest does not refer to officials in the Roman Catholic Church. Priest may refer to any pagan or Christian person who officiates at the altar.

**We believe that a few men may have gotten overly zealous and carried the persecution to much greater lengths than the opposition intended. Because we knew they didn't understand what we stood for, it was easy to forgive them.

Afeef, Michael, Moses, and Mary are in front of the tent in Shekka that got the bullet.

CHAPTER 13

STUDENTS WITHOUT A SCHOOL

The permit to hold public evangelistic meetings in Shekka during the summer of 1948 never materialized, but the summer was not wasted. Moses, Michael, Wayne and I made countless visits and gave numerous Bible studies. Besides that, the boys held three afternoon meetings a week for the children of the village. About 75 youngsters attended their special meetings. Michael set the children on the edge of their seats with his dramatized, character-building stories. He used the Sabbath School picture rolls to help the children visualize the Bible stories. Moses taught them music. Soon the kids were singing Adventist choruses and telling their version of the Bible stories all over Shekka.

The parents were so pleased with what their children were learning that they wanted the Adventists to stay the year around. "Why not start a school?" they pleaded. Such a bold move had never crossed our minds, but once it was suggested, we liked the idea. EDUCATION! The most practical way to wedge the gospel message into the hearts of the children, who, in turn, would teach it to their parents. Why hadn't we thought of it first? Perhaps we weren't supposed to—people would place more value on an education if they had to work to get a school started.

We agreed to work on getting a permit to open an elementary school; Moses agreed to stay on and teach. The mission committee shared our excitement and contracted with two young lady teachers to help Wayne and Moses. Given our former experience with getting permits, I don't know why we were ever so naive as to hope we could secure a school permit in time to begin school the last of September, but there seems to be a thin line between faith and presumption. We had some of both.

Afeef and Wayne worked on getting the school permit while Moses and our village friends looked over buildings which might be rented to house the school. We, the mission, and our Shekka friends were so confident that the school permit would be summarily granted that Wayne hired a carpenter to build school desks. Unfortunately, the carpenter chose to do his work on the sidewalk outside of his shop. Seeing these new desks being completed became a hornet under the robe of the village priest. His resentment intensified every day as he passed the carpenter's shop, observing the objects representing our intentions. Secretly he and the bishop connived together to stop us from opening a school as they had connived to stop our meetings.

When autumn arrived, we were still without the school permit. Given the superb reputation our schools in the Beirut area enjoyed, this astonished us all. In faith we had selected a building, had it inspected for safety by the government engineer and for health by the government health officer. We got their stamp of approval. Wayne, as principal, had presented his diplomas, letters of recommendation and other papers. But still there remained that illusive "something". We simply couldn't understand the delay. We always seemed to be chasing rainbows that evaporated before reality materialized. The reason? We hadn't yet conceived the influence and power the bishop held over the government officials. Politics and religion blurred into one and the same

STUDENTS WITHOUT A SCHOOL

thing. Since we didn't represent the established religion, we didn't get the permit.

The families who had sponsored the idea of our starting a school, now faced an angry priest who refused to enroll their children in his school. This posed a problem. The seven boys who were disallowed the church's school did not want to go to the government school, either. They felt the academic standards there were too low, and that they would not receive the instructions they needed to enable them to pass the government tests. Without that qualifying certificate, they could not proceed with their high school education. Therefore, the priest's decree left seven students without a school.

Moses solved their problem by renting a seaside cottage where he could tutor the boys privately. They were elated with this solution. Thus the retributive justice that the priest had thought to inflict upon the families who chose religious independence, didn't penalize their teenage children after all.

About this time, we decided that we too should move from our comfortable house in Tripoli to Shekka where interest in the message was still strong. We hoped to find a house with a living room large enough to hold cottage meetings. If we couldn't hold public evangelistic meetings, we would have private ones. The interested people would hear the message, just as the boys would have a school.* Consequently, the mission hired Moses permanently as a translator for us and a tutor for the students without a school.

Since we did not get the school permit, the mission transferred the lady teachers elsewhere and used the desks in other schools.

Hope springs eternal for those who trust in God. Our faith in God's guidance had certainly been reinforced that summer by His remarkable deliverance from a show-down with death in the wheat field. Now all we needed was for God to direct us to a rental in Shekka. We supposed that in the privacy of our own home, no one could keep us from preaching the gospel! Or could they?

*In the spring, all the boys passed their government exams. Moses had tutored them well. Philip, Afeef's younger brother, went on to Middle East College where he became a Seventh-day Adventist. The others remained good friends and may have accepted Christianity later. Through the years of civil disturbances in Lebanon, we have lost contact with them.

CHAPTER 14

"PLEASE, GOD, SPARE THE CHILD"

Summer drifted into mid-October. I was anxiously awaiting the birth of my baby. I hoped the child would be normal in spite of the miserable pregnancy that had caused me to lose so much weight. Perhaps my discomfort was intensified by our having to camp down at the college part time while Wayne was drilling the well. Then Ronnie's bout with malaria had strained my nerves. Our struggle with the forces of evil in Shekka during the summer months caused additional stress. Now I worried that Mary would have to return to college before the baby arrived. Then who would look after Ronnie while I was in the hospital? Added to that was the concern of being without a home. We had given notice to the owner of our Tripoli duplex that we would be moving November 1, but we still had not found housing in Shekka. In truth, there weren't many houses in Shekka to rent.

I felt apprehensive, like something was wrong, when I went into the hospital October 17, Wayne's 25th birthday. There was no celebration that day—just a day-long vigil waiting for the child to be born. About midnight they discovered the baby was breach and couldn't be delivered easily. Some consultations and an hour and a half later, they got the baby. When he didn't cry, I knew immediately that my fears were justified. With some effort the doctor finally got the baby to gasp for air.

Nothing sounded better to my ear—his cry was an omen of hope.

After I was taken back to my room the doctor came in and talked to me. "Honestly, I can't promise that the baby will be normal. I fear he was without a proper supply of oxygen for too long. He may be spastic or have other complications. We'll just have to wait and see."

I didn't need to hear that. I was already in so much physical pain. Through the whole 24-hour ordeal, I had had no medication. I was weak and emotionally exhausted too. In my distress I cried out, "Oh, God, why this? Haven't we endured enough? Please spare the baby and let him be normal. How can we carry on our work for You if he is a basket case? Please look after that little bundle of flesh in the nursery tonight and undo the damage that might have been done during my pregnancy and his delivery. Amen."

Early the next morning Wayne was back at the hospital. "What shall we name the baby?" he asked exuding excitement. Wayne didn't know what the doctor had told me and I hadn't the courage to divulge it.

"I'm not up to thinking of a permanent name for a baby that might not be..." I left the sentence dangling. I wouldn't face the problem, not yet.

The nurse brought the baby in, and we looked him over. He seemed absolutely perfect except for his head. "Look," Wayne laughed, "this boy looks like a Swede that's been in a big fight. His face is swollen and his head is a little misshaped. Poor little guy. He had a rough time getting here, and you had a rough time delivering him. He looks so different from Ronnie. She had dark hair and perfect facial features. This baby is blond and, and, ah, ruddy looking."

"PLEASE, GOD, SPARE THE CHILD"

"Yes, he is," I toyed absent mindedly with the baby's little fingers. "I was just thinking, this child is born in the Bible lands. Let's name him after a Bible character—like Joseph, or..."

"DAVID! That would be a good name for him. The Bible says that David was ruddy and fair. Maybe something like this baby. And, after all, we want him to become a man after God's own heart. Let's call him David."

So the baby was called David Wayne Olson. Every day Ronnie came to see her little "bruver".

The week was filled with apprehension. I kept waiting for complications to show up in my son; Wayne kept looking for a house in Shekka. Friday, five days after David's birth, Wayne returned with the good news. Good news? Well, sort of. He had found a rental. It was the back part of a woodworking shop right off the main street. It had a minuscule bath and kitchen, but Wayne promised to modernize them for me. It had two bedrooms—one in which we could store the chairs and evangelistic equipment, and the other one for the family. This would be PRIMITIVE living, but we had promised God that we would make sacrifices. At least now we were guaranteed a roof over our heads. Besides, the house had one special feature we had prayed for—a living/dining room combination that was large enough for cottage meetings. Nothing about the place really satisfied the family needs, but it was ideal for small worship services.

Sabbath morning I awakened feeling very uncomfortable. It wasn't just the concern for the baby or the unsatisfactory housing situation I was facing; I was plainly SICK! By noon I was running a fever of 105 and had become delirious. I kept insisting that the nurses get the pesky donkeys out of the corners of my room. The doctors knew my delivery had not gone well, and now they feared that a serious infection was making rapid progress. Why, the doctors wondered, hadn't the infection shown up sooner? Suddenly, surprisingly, it had appeared after five days and stripped me of my senses. Missionaries from Beirut came to see me, and I didn't know any of them. I blubbered nonsense because the high temperature kept me hallucinating.

On Sunday suspicious symptoms showed up in David. He turned yellow; his stools were pasty gray. The doctors checked me; I also was turning a dandelion shade of yellow.

"Wow! She has a REAL case of infectious hepatitis!" Doctor Boyes told Wayne. "She can't go home until we get a handle on this and neither can the baby."

Wayne, Michael, Moses, and Mary moved our belongings out to Shekka. Then Mary and Michael returned to college; the Shammases took charge of Ronnie. Wayne painted, installed a make-shift shower in a corner of the bathroom, and made a sink in the kitchen from packing boxes and molded zinc.

David and I arrived home on a Friday. Our friends in Shekka brought in food and helped wherever they could. Sabbath the house was crowded with guests, so I forced myself out of bed and dressed to greet them. I surprised Wayne and myself when I fainted, but that convinced me that I should follow the doctor's advice and stay mostly in bed for the next four weeks. I didn't understand enough about hepatitis to realize the debilitating effects of the disease. My enlarged liver caused me pain, and the fever had left made me weak.

Even when no visitors were around, I still had two-year-old Ronnie with which to cope. She was a delightfully happy child, but keeping an active one like her out of the baby's buggy was a challenge beyond my

"PLEASE, GOD, SPARE THE CHILD"

physical capacity. When she wasn't in the buggy smashing the baby, she dumped the puppy in with him, or forced another bottle into his mouth. She very nearly loved David to death. Perhaps David owes his life to the Shammas girls who took Ronnie to their home every day. Ronnie loved their pampering, and it helped David survive until I was well enough to control the situation.

We began meetings in our home in Shekka almost immediately. We had no choice. People dropped by any time during the day and night to discuss Biblical topics. So in order to have any time in which to care for the kids and the premises, we spread the word that we would have three meetings per week and would accept visitors during the afternoons. This freed our mornings to wash, clean, shop, etc.

Within a few weeks we settled into a routine that we could live with. Three nights per week 20 to 30 people gathered in our living/dining room for the Bible study. We owned an oldfashioned couch whose back was hinged to the seat in such a way that it could be laid out flat to make into a bed. This comfy couch was respectfully relegated to the shuckseeya (the older, elite men) of the village while simple, straight-backed chairs sufficed for the others.

One night, four very large men sat down on our couch to enjoy the meeting. I noticed the couch creak and complain as the men shifted their weight about from time to time. About halfway through Wayne's discourse, we heard a loud crack, then a big THUD! The couch collapsed to the floor leaving the shuckseeya caught within its folds. Their feet and hands were aimed at the ceiling and their rotund bodies squashed together vice-like. What a lot of grunting and groaning, pushing and pulling it took to extricate those heavy men from their trap. I thought it was so hilarious that I had to go into the bedroom to smother my giggles. How the rest of the group kept from thigh-slapping laughter was more than I could imagine. But they did. They were too courteous to laugh at the embarrassing mishap. The next day was a different story. The whole village knew about the couch that snapped and trapped the elite of the town. That joke was good enough to last everyone a whole month.

Since our old, second-hand, recovered couch was the only comfortable piece of furniture that we owned, we had to repair it immediately. Wayne went to the wood shop on the front side of our house and came back dragging a piece of lumber large enough to support Solomon's temple. He removed the broken two by four and wedged in the "log". The davenport wasn't quite as comfortable anymore, but it could now support a ton of weight.

Thanksgiving arrived, and we were thankful. We had survived injury or death in the wheat field, David had been spared and showed no evidence of physical, neurological, or mental damage, I was healthy again, and the meetings were going well. We spent the day with the other expatriates in Beirut. Thanksgiving was the one "high day" of the year when all of the Adventist missionary families (about 60 of us) of whatever nationality got together.

Close on the heels of Thanksgiving came Christmas. This would be our second one in North Lebanon. That year the Arthur Keough family thoughtfully invited us to spend a few days with them and his parents in Beirut. Sabbath after church, we drove down to Beirut and moved into one of Keough's bedrooms. Dinner that evening was very special. Dora Keough was of English extraction, and she spread a traditional English Christmas feast on her table-tarts, puddings, yule-log cake,

"PLEASE, GOD, SPARE THE CHILD"

and other foods I had never seen. Since we were of Scandinavian descent, the contrasts in foods, were new and exciting for us. Yet, one sacred strand binds all Christians everywhere together—our focus on the birth of Jesus. The Christmas story had more meaning than ever to our families that year. Each of us had a new baby boy—Keoughs had Alger, and we had David.

Sunday began beautifully. Ronnie played with Norma, Keough's daughter who was her age, while we adults chatted, cared for our babies, and prepared more food. After lunch, however, David became violently ill with vomiting and diarrhea. We rushed him to emergency, got medication, and went home to Shekka. We supposed that David would recover quickly with the sulfa drug, but he did not. Once again our prayer was, "Please, God, spare the child." We could not have imagined then how many times we would make that same petition in the next few months.

CHAPTER 15

SHEKKA IS NO MECCA

Mecca is the city in Saudi Arabia where Mohammed, prophet of the Islamic faith, was born. He was religiously inclined and, in solitude, meditated upon God and creation. Some tenets of his beliefs were formulated from concepts he learned from both Judaism and Christianity. Mohammed taught that there is one creator God, Allah, that man has a moral and religious responsibility toward God and man, and that there is a judgment awaiting mankind on the day of resurrection. His new theology conflicted with that of the pagan leaders of his day, so he was forced to seek refuge in Medina. However, by the year 630 A.D. his following had grown to the extent that it was possible for him to return to Mecca and set up his headquarters there. This time the Arabs flocked to his banner, and Mecca became the pilgrimage goal for every devout Moslem. Mecca is the center of Islam. Somehow we felt we could move into Shekka, make it our Mecca, and set up our headquarters there. But it was not to be.

During the first few months we lived in Shekka the opposition hadn't figured out how to stop our progress, but they were just waiting in the wings. In January they struck again.

Afeef warned us. He overheard a conversation that indicated the police would be coming to our home, sitting in as spies, and then arresting us on whatever pretense they could concoct. "When the police come, treat them very courteously, Mrs. Olson," Afeef suggested. "Have something ready to serve them. You know it is an unwritten law among the Arabs that people cannot be enemies when they have just shared food."

I was galled to think anyone would have the effrontery to come into our home, spy on us, and then trump up reasons to arrest us in order to stop our meetings. But by now, I had come to expect anything. My next reaction, of course, was to pray about it. Then I looked forward to implementing my plan on the police. Maybe my high school drama lessons would come in handy now. I knew enough Arabic by this time to feel confident of my speech. I also believed that, with the help of God, I could entice the police into eating some cookies.

I pulled my last batch of cookies out of the oven at meeting time, shared some with the group, and then waited nervously for our "guests". Sure enough, about ten minutes after the meeting began that night, there was a knock on the door. The audience tensed but knew how to play their part—they continued to look intently at Wayne and pretended not to hear the persistent knock nor see the police when they entered.

I walked to the door, flung it open wide and in my best Arabic said, "What a privilege it is for us to have two men of the law come to HEAR lessons from the BIBLE!!" (Insinuating, of course, that they had come with no ulterior motives.)

The men stuttered something, but I completely ignored them. I shook their hands vigorously and pushed them gently into chairs. I didn't want to give them a chance to think or talk. I intended to confuse them with my overwhelming reception. "Here," I whispered, "I just baked some cookies. Please honor me by eating some." Police are not used to such royal treatment, so this completely bewildered them.

SHEKKA IS NO MECCA

The spicy aroma from the kitchen had drifted into the dining area where they sat, tantalizing their senses. Like most men tempted with food, they indulged. I suggested that a glass of orange juice might help quench their thirst, so I slyly poured a glass of liquid gold and handed it to them. Soon they had emptied the plate of cookies and the pitcher of juice.

Then they realized they had been tricked. But since I had lavished Arab hospitality upon them, they couldn't just get up and leave conveniently, either. Such bad manners would have been the gossip of the town the next day. Therefore, they were obliged to sit and listen to the Bible message. It did them good too. They went out and testified, "Adventists really seem to be Christians. Their whole message was centered around Christ and His love." This naturally angered those who had employed them. This was not what they had been asked to do or say.

Hoping for better luck the next time, the opposition engaged two different police to do what the first two failed to do. They too arrived about ten minutes after the meeting began. They put up a little more resistance than their predecessors, but they had no resistance to my cookies; they left only a few crumbs on the plate. They were embarrassed over their defeat—but what could they do? God had confounded their wills. They too listened carefully to the service and left declaring that we very well might be the best Christians in Shekka. This was not what the opposition had wanted them to do, either.

The evening of the next meeting found me finishing another batch of oatmeal cookies. Two more police arrived on the scene, and I went through my "come-in-sit-down-eat-it-up" routine. I had perfected my act by now, and God never allowed them to resist. Again the police went out with glowing reports of what they had seen and heard.

By now, the opposition had run through the whole gamut of the police force in Shekka, and they had all come away from our house with a positive report. So, our enemies gave up that plan. After all, what if one of those policemen converted to Adventism. It would be their fault for sending him to us.

For the moment, things had come to an impasse, but we knew there remained a smoldering volcano just waiting to erupt. What happened next surprised even us.

Jazmeen, our little Bedouin servant girl, was late coming to work on Monday morning. I proceeded with my laundry as usual and had it nearly all hung up on the veranda by the time she arrived. She approached me hesitatingly, a wild fear clouding her face.

"Hi, Jazmeen. I'm glad you're here," I said, trying to put her at ease. "We still have to scrub down all of the floors and disinfect them. After the weekend meetings and the Saturday night socials, our house is always a shambles. You're coming to help us means so much to me. I'm so thankful for you, Jazmeen."

"And, ah, I'm thankful for you, Mrs. Olson," Jazmeen said with a bit of tremor in her voice. "But I don't know if I should come here any more. The devil tried to kill me last night as I crossed the railroad tracks. I got away, but he called after me, 'If you ever stay for the meetings again, I'll get you. You must have nothing to do with Adventist Christianity."

"What? I can't believe what you just said! I mean, I know you don't lie, Jazmeen, but this is so, so bizarre. Could this be your imagination? Or did some real person dress up and say and do things to scare you into believing it was the devil? I don't think the devil would appear in person and do such extraterrestrial things. He's more subtle than that—or so I thought. Just sit down, Jazmeen, and let's talk this thing through." I dropped my laundry basket, collapsed into a chair on the veranda, and Jazmeen slid onto another.

"No, Madame, we know the devil when we see him. None of my people have ever become Christians, and we probably never should. The devil will only make trouble for the people we join."

"But how can you be sure, Jazmeen? How can you know it was the devil?"

Jazmeen took a deep breath, and her eyes looked glassy. "Last night the devil was a greenish color, he was about seven feet tall, he wore a prickly hood, and had a slashing tail. He grabbed me by the throat with bumpy gloves, shook me, then tried to choke me. I pleaded for my life, and after a long struggle he released me. But I had to promise never to stay at your house for another meeting. See here," she said, pointing to her throat. "Look at the scratches and marks he left."

I examined the plentiful physical evidence left around Jazmeen's throat. Whoever or whatever had caught her, had certainly done a number on her. I tried to console this frightened young girl, but I had no explanation for the phenomenon. My mind drifted back to the summer when I had colporteured in Minnesota and encountered a spiritualist. She possessed powers that electrified me and shattered credulity. I had tried to bury those discomforting memories, but now they flashed back. If what Jazmeen was saying was true, Satan himself had arrived in Shekka to render a most impressive and terrifying performance.

Wayne and I discussed the matter at length and agreed with Jazmeen not to share this information with anyone. Jazmeen continued to work for us, but she never attended another meeting.

The next Monday morning, Moses arrived before we had finished breakfast. "Hi, Moses. What brings you out so early?" Wayne asked cheerily. But Moses, who was by nature a bit reserved, seemed to be having unusual trouble communicating. "We surely had a good attendance last night, didn't we?" Wayne continued trying to jump-start Moses.

"I don't know how to tell you this," Moses began slowly, "but the devil attacked me last night on the way home and tried to kill me with a huge stone."

"WHAT?" Wayne and I exclaimed in unison. "Not you! Tell us about it."

"Well, I left the meeting a little later than usual, as you will remember. I took the usual route home—to the soap factory down by the sea and across the soccer field. When I got to the middle of the field, a large stone came out of nowhere and landed right at my feet. If it would have hit my head, it would have killed me. I knew the stone was too large to have been thrown by any human. Besides, there was no human around anywhere! I was so shocked I just stood there awhile and then raced home. Knowing that there were no stones that size anywhere near the soccer field, I went back there this morning to see if the devil really had hurtled a stone to kill me. Sure enough, there is a large stone in the exact spot where it landed last night. It is even larger than I suspected—probably 13 inches in diameter."

Wayne and I were agape; the toast stuck in our throats. Moses expected some response. I poked Wayne, hoping he had recovered sufficiently to dribble a few appropriate words. What would have been appropriate at that time was a matter of conjecture. At last Moses

SHEKKA IS NO MECCA

made a fitting proposal. "Walk with me down to the soccer field and see the stone for yourselves."

Wayne and I left breakfast and walked to the open field with Moses. There was indeed a very large, lone stone in the middle of the field, lying in the indentation it had made when it landed. It had not rolled or turned—just dropped there from nowhere.

Now we thought it appropriate to tell Moses of Jazmeen's experience. The two episodes seemed definitely related. But Moses, our translator, couldn't skip the meeting as Jazmeen did. After our next meeting, we prayed fervently for Moses protection. And that same phenomenon never happened again. The devil, however, had an even more frightening experience for Moses.

A few nights later, Moses locked his doors and went to bed as usual. Just as he was drifting to sleep, someone grasped him by the throat and tried to strangle him. Moses struggled to get free but felt himself passing out. He breathed a quick prayer, and God forced "the thing" to release him. After Moses could breath normally again, he arose, turned on the lights, and searched his house thoroughly. He believed there was a very strong antagonist in the house with him. He inspected every nook and cranny, but there was no one.

Moses lay down in a cold sweat, knowing he was having another encounter with the devil. He spent the rest of the night in prayer. The next day he told us of his night of terror. "I wished I would have been wrestling with the angel of the Lord like Jacob instead of an agent of the devil," Moses told us.

"Of course that would have been better, but we know that God is with us as surely as He was with Jacob. He'll subdue the devil for us," Wayne said confidently. "By the way, Moses, have you done anything different recently that might have incensed the devil?"

"Let's see," Moses paused to reflect. "Well, I've spent a lot of time reading Steps to Christ. Would that rile him?"

"Who knows? The devil surely wouldn't want you coming closer to Jesus, and that book has a tendency to do it. I'm sure the devil would like to scare you into leaving Shekka. You have a big influence on your students, and you are my right hand man. We need you here, Moses, and the devil knows that. Let's pray that God will break his power."

The three of us fasted and prayed that day. God granted our petition, and the devil never made another attempt on Moses' life. Once more we saw God interrupt Satan's plans. We hoped that now we could continue our work in peace. PEACE? That word was foreign for us in Shekka.

The people seemed to know our every move. Wednesday evenings Wayne studied with a fisherman and his family down by the seashore. On this moonlit night, Wayne took his usual route—skirting the soccer field where Moses had escaped being hit by the stone and walking on the road directly in front of the olive oil soap factory. As he turned the corner, his eye caught a slight movement in the archway of the main gate. A shiver ran up Wayne's spine. Was someone waiting for him? Rumors that someone would soon kill Wayne had circulated in the village, but Wayne had ignored them up until this moment. The situation for murder was ideal. Wayne was alone, he could be killed with no one seeing or knowing, and his body thrown into the sea.

"Lord, help me," Wayne pleaded. "Give me wisdom, please."

SHEKKA IS NO MECCA

Though Wayne was still trembling, he felt a peace settling into his soul. Feeling no need to delay the encounter, Wayne walked directly to the doorway. "Hello, in there," he called. "I am Wayne Olson, the Adventist minister. Who is there?" Wayne extended his hand into the shadows. There was some surprised muttering, but no hand reached out to his. A bad omen.

A long pause. Wayne prayed some more. "I, ah, don't know if we've met but I'd like to know all the people in this town and become their friend. There's a lot of nice people here." Wayne was trying to curry favor and gain time.

"And some not so nice," the man sneered. "Why have you come here to preach your American heathen stuff? No wonder the priest hates you."

"But we aren't heathen, and the gospel of Jesus Christ isn't American. It's a message for the whole world. God loves all of us—you, me..."

"Yeah? What do you know about Jesus Christ? You don't even know who the Virgin Mary was?"

"Of course, I do," Wayne protested. "She was the most righteous woman that ever lived. She was so saintly that God chose her to bear His son, Jesus. Oh, we certainly do believe in the Virgin Mary!"

The man stepped out of the shadows. "That wasn't what I was told. What else do you teach?"

"I don't know what you've been told, but I believe you have been misinformed about us. May I just take a few minutes to explain my faith in Jesus?"

"Got nothin' else scheduled for tonight," the man laughed, a slight hint of embarrassment catching his voice. "Shoot!" Perhaps that was a poor choice of words for such a man.

Inspired by the Holy Spirit, Wayne presented the gospel so simply, so appealingly to this man, that he was moved to the core. "You have convinced me that you are a true Christian. No one ever told me about God and Jesus as you have. Please pray for me, Sir," the tremulous voice whispered as he fumbled for Wayne's hand.

The next day the rumor circulated in the village that the man at the factory would have been paid had he murdered Wayne. Wayne's friendliness had pre-empted the plot. We were never able to prove if the rumor was true, but it seemed strange to us that anyone in the village would even know about this encounter since Wayne never told anyone but me. Who told the villagers about the incident at the oil factory? Wayne never knew, nor did he see the man again.

Our small home had become central station to so many people that it was like a public building. This was not good or healthy for the children. Their naps and feeding times were constantly interrupted, and they were exposed to every flu, cold, or dysentery germ in circulation. They were constantly on and off penicillin, sulfa drugs, and other medication. There was not room in our one small bedroom with it's furniture for them to play. The dining/living room was always swarming with activity, and the kitchen was only large enough for the cook. But the pattern was set and impossible to break at this point in time.

Besides trying to manage a home and family and operate a meeting center, I made several house calls a day to women. Wayne and Moses made house calls too but kept trying to contrive new methods of outreach. They devised the plan of having a monthly tea to which they would invite leading government officials and other important people in the area. This socializing broke down prejudice and set up good lines of communication, but it also added to my work load—not to mention the money it siphoned off my monthly food budget. I was fatigued but happy that this public relations effort was effective.

The people living in the mountain villages heard of the Adventists who had come to live in Shekka. They heard how we had been denied permits that should legally have been granted. They heard of the plot in the wheat field and wondered why we aroused the indignation of the clergy. They became suspicious of their church leaders. They came down to Shekka to learn more about us. They talked to the villagers who sang our praises, intensifying the interest of the mountain folks. Representatives from many towns came to our home, making requests that we come and teach them. Interestingly enough, nearly all of these requests were tendered by well educated, refined people. They were not content to be fed tradition anymore. They wanted to read and hear the Bible for themselves. They came from Tannureen, Enfeh, Amuin, Taboora, Halba, Farhazier, Rutga, Afesdik, and Bishmizeen—nine new towns!

When the mission sent us to North Lebanon, they hoped that we could establish a base for preaching the exciting message of salvation. They anxiously watched our progress since earlier mission attempts had failed. No one, in his wildest dreams, had ever expected the flood of invitations that now inundated us. General Conference and mission officers came to see for themselves the amazing interest that had deluged us in less than two years. They agreed that we needed help and promised to send us some college students when summer vacation came. In the meantime, the best we could do was to keep contact with the interested villagers. We hoped they would wait for three months until we would have personnel to send to them.

MIDGE IN LEBANON

Shekka did not turn out to be the Mecca we had hoped it would. It obviously was not the place to establish our headquarters in North Lebanon. But what transpired there set the stage for the future of God's work. The persecution and the denial of rightful permits had sent flames of curiosity bounding into the mountain villages. There the light of truth would settle and never be extinguished.

CHAPTER 16

THROUGH THE DARK VALLEY

The year 1949 proved to be one of the most hectic of our lives. The devil plagued us in every conceivable way: his personal encounter with Moses and his appearance to Jazmeen, the opposition to our work, the threats on our lives, and the stress of our children's poor health caused by our impossible living conditions. We would have gladly changed the latter, but the devil had us locked into the housing situation—the only way we could hold meetings in Shekka was to have them in our home since we could not secure a permit for public meetings.

Besides the flow of human traffic that exposed the children to every popular germ abroad, the house itself was inadequately small and situated in an unhealthful location. Our building fronted the main highway between Beirut and Tripoli. Our apartment was in the back half of the building, but my little socialite Ronnie liked to run around to the front to "see the peoples". The danger of her getting out onto the road and getting hit by a car kept me on edge. The front part of the building contained a large woodwork shop. The scream of the electric saws in the workshop during the daytime grated on my nerves.

The front door and only accessible side of our apartment led out onto an uncovered veranda. By April the heat waves bouncing off that cement slab kept us dripping in perspiration. The humidity was high since we lived only an eighth of a mile from the Mediterranean Sea. With the heat came the flies and mosquitos who practiced their reproduction programs in the neighbor's chicken yard just beyond the narrow stretch of dirt separating our yards. Oh how I longed for a more suitable place to raise my children.

My complaints were many and perhaps even justifiable. However, there was the flip side too. We had been inundated with requests for cottage meetings. We had prayed that God would open doors of opportunity for us, but we hadn't expected so many. For Moses, Wayne, and me to just touch base with all the interests until we had time to arrange Bible studies with the people was a challenge in itself. Since we couldn't answer all the Macedonian calls, we asked God to guide us in our selection. He definitely pointed us to the foothill town of Farhazier.

April 11 became a red-letter day in our book of memories—that was when we began meetings in the Akar home in Farhazier. Once a week we drove to the end of the road and carried the children up to the top of the hill where the three Akar families occupied commodious houses. They were educated, hospitable people, and it was a pleasure to socialize and study the Bible with them. We also enjoyed breathing the pure mountain air. After inhaling that for a few hours, I didn't want to return to our cramped, moldy-smelling home down in Shekka. However, since we felt we still needed a base in Shekka we stayed there.

Wayne came up with a brilliant idea that we supposed would solve our insect problem. On May 9 he purchased some 100% DDT, mixed it with kerosene, and sprayed the walls of the house. After that not a fly or mosquito set foot or wing inside our house without dropping dead in seconds. (It was not until some years later that we learned DDT was a carcinogen.)

In June Middle East College was out for the summer and help arrived. Michael Kebbas returned to work with us. We sent him up to Rutga to confirm some interests there. Farris Bishi, a ministerial intern, went to Farhazier to translate for Jim and Carolyn Russell, teachers from Middle East College on loan to us for the summer. Moses stayed in Shekka with us. Now the work was equitably distributed, and we could breath more easily.

Ronnalee's third birthday was July 20 so we had a little party for her. Nine-month-old David whizzed around in his walker trying to get hold of the pretty papers to chew on. I purposely kept him in the walker to keep him cleaner, safer, and healthier. I thought I had been reasonably successful at this, but on July 23, dysentery struck David with a vengeance. Diarrhea and vomiting for a baby is very dangerous during the hot summer months—dehydration can mean death within a few hours. We rushed him to the doctor in Tripoli immediately.

After three days, we realized that the sulfa drugs were not effectively curing our son. July 26 we transferred him to the American University Hospital in Beirut. He was already dangerously dehydrated. They poked large needles into his abdomen and bloated him with a water solution. The poor baby cried in his pain and struggled to free himself from the torture. I could hardly bear to stand over his bed and hold him tightly while he suffered. Still the vomiting and bloody stools persisted.

The children's wards were filled with dysentery victims that summer. Every morning as I walked down the hallway, I counted the number of sheets pulled over the little dead bodies. I empathized with the parents whose hearts were breaking. I knew David wasn't getting any better and that he might be the next victim. David survived a week; then Dr. Nachman told us to take him out of the hospital and up to the mountains. There was nothing more that he or the hospital could do for him. David's only chance, a very slim one at that, was to get out of the coastal heat to delay the dehydration process. Then if we could feed him some nourishing fluids that he could keep down, he might possibly recover. Dr. Nachman made no promises, nor, significantly, any future appointments. We understood clearly, then, that David's demise was eminent.

Mrs. Haddad heard about the tragedy we faced, and immediately sent word for us to come up to Beit Meri to stay with her. Where else would we rather go? She was like my second mother. Victoria was also skilled in child care and practical nursing. So to the Haddad home we went.

Mrs. Haddad cried when she saw our baby, "Oh, he is so very ill. Only God can save him." We knew she was right.

While Wayne and I had spent our days and nights in the hospital with David, Ronnalee stayed in Shekka with the Shammases. But we missed the little punkin' so much that Wayne went to Shekka and got her. Then we discovered that she too was sick. When we got her up in the cool mountains of Beit Meri she responded quite rapidly to the change of climate, medication, and diet of Mrs. Haddad. She became her chipper little self again and a source of comfort to us. What a blessing to have one healthy child. Our little boy was just wasting away.

On Sabbath, August 6, the Kricks visited us in Beit Meri. Mrs. Krick was a nurse of keen insight. After she observed David for awhile, she put her arms around me.

THROUGH THE DARK VALLEY

"Midge, you know there really isn't much hope for him, don't you? Are you praying that God's will be done?"

"Well, almost. I don't want to loose him, but he has suffered so much. I am told that being without proper nourishment for so long could cause permanent physical or mental damage to him. I wouldn't want him to live if he would be handicapped for the rest of his life..."

"That's right. Leave it in the hands of God," Mrs. Krick advised giving me another hug. As she turned aside, I noted she dabbed tears from her eyes. I had already shed grams of tears myself, but it was consoling to know she also cared. Jesus wept. Was He weeping with me too?

That Sabbath evening Victoria, Wayne and I had a prayer service. We prayed that if it was God's will that David should die, to please take him quickly. It didn't make us feel any better, but we had come to grips with reality. None of us could bear to see the baby suffer anymore. Even the nurse who came to give him his daily vitamin shots complained that there was not enough unused muscle tissue left for her to give his injections.

After Ronnie went to bed, the house was unusually quiet. Each of us moved silently about trying to cope in our own way with the possible death of David. Mrs. Haddad cooked a thick brew from barley. Then, with an eye dropper we dripped a spoonful of barley water into David's parched mouth every half hour. He swallowed it but remained in a stupor.

That night, as I knelt by my bed, the strangest experience of my life took place. Was it a vision? A dream? A visit from an angel? I do not know. I even hesitate to relate the story, but because of the impact it had upon us, our decisions, and the mission work in North Lebanon, I feel I must.

As I prayed, suddenly a nicely dressed man appeared on the other side of my bed. He was gazing into a large coffin in front of him. Then I seemed to be standing beside him, looking into the coffin too. There I saw an old man, appropriately wrinkled for his 80-some years. He had all the features of my son, right down to the curly hair—except that it was gray. I knew it was the body of David; but whatever could this mean I wondered.

Then the man spoke. "The adult body symbolizes that your son will live out his normal life span, if time should last. He will get worse and everyone will despair for his life. But he will LIVE! Now wait!" he continued, holding up his hand. "I have more to tell you. Because of the stress you have endured these past two years, there have been suggestions that you may wish to move to another country. Do not go. God has many souls in the El-Khoura district just waiting to be taught. Soon people will be asking for baptism. Establish the work there." (This reminded me of the message given Paul in Acts 18: 9, 10. God told Paul that he would not get hurt if he stayed in Corinth and preached because "I have many people in this city.") "Yet another point is still puzzling you. As you look at this coffin you are wondering if the Lord will delay His coming until your son is an old man. No! God does not want to delay His coming. It is up to His people; if they do their work faithfully, Jesus will come before your son is an old man. Be comforted."

The next moment there was NOTHING. The 3-D images had all vanished. It had been so real, so consoling, that gentle voice—I wanted to call it all back.

As the scene faded, Wayne spoke, "Midge, are you all right? You've been on your knees a long time. And, ah, the expression on your face—you look so content. Were you asleep?"

THROUGH THE DARK VALLEY

"Oh, Wayne," I said, rising in a state of ecstacy. "Wasn't it marvelous?"

"What was marvelous?" he asked, obviously perplexed.

"What the man said. David will get worse, but he will live."

"Midge, David can't get worse and live. He is so weak now that he can't even cry. What are you talking about? What man?"

"The man who was just here," I answered nearly bursting with exuberance. Then I realized from Wayne's expression that he was pointedly oblivious to what had transpired. I stopped talking then, disappointed that he didn't share the mystery. Now how was I going to explain to someone who was in the same room with me, that I had SEEN and HEARD something? "He's, well, he's gone now," I murmured, fumbling for words. "But you did hear him talk!"

"No, Midge, I didn't. Are you sure you are not hallucinating?"

I sat down on the edge of the bed and recalled the vivid scene to my mind. "Hallucinating? Imagining? Nerves? I know that's what people will think if I tell them. Dreaming? No, I wasn't asleep. I can tell what I saw, but I don't know why it should have happened to me. If this is from God, everything the man said should come to pass. It seems completely preposterous, but there WAS a man, and he DID talk to me." Then I rehearsed for Wayne the points he made: 1) David would get worse, but live; 2) we should not leave Lebanon but move to the El-Koura district; 3) there would be a harvest of souls from that area; and 4) God did not want His people to delay His coming by neglecting His work.

MIDGE IN LEBANON

Wayne sank onto his bed, dumbfounded. Finally he spoke. "Midge, I do think God was trying to tell us something. I know we both thought it would be nice to move to Jordan. Now I'm convinced we should move to Farhazier and work there while we wait for the predictions to come true. We have submitted David's life to the will of God. If he lives, as the 'Man' said, that will be the first proof to the authenticity of this, this, whatever it was you saw and heard."

"I think you're right, Wayne. If it's from God, everything will come to pass. But let's not tell anyone else about this—whatever it was. Who would believe it, anyway? I can hardly believe it myself. I feel so unworthy of this communication. It's scary."

"I'm sure anyone would feel the same way, Midge. But God knows about our perplexities. By revealing a few secrets and giving advice to us at this time, He meant to encourage and comfort us. This was His special touch of love. It shows how closely our Heavenly Father associates himself with His earthly family. God answers people's prayers through impressions or dreams all the time."

The next day Wayne shared my experience with Mrs. Haddad. Immediately she was impressed that it was a message from God and that we should accept it as such. Reluctantly, she agreed to keep our secret. She believed that we should tell others so that when the predictions came true everyone would know of God's personal interest in His people and His work.

That morning we felt God's lingering presence about us so we decided to fast and pray. We wanted to keep our fine of communication with heaven open.

David got worse as predicted, and our hearts ached as we watched him struggle for fife. Finally we bundled the limp little body up and took him over to Dr. Nachman's home. The doctor was amazed to see that David still lived. He just sat there folding and unfolding his hands, staring at David. "I have nothing more to tell you. I know of nothing else to do," he admitted lamely.

"What about trying some evaporated milk instead of the special baby formulas?" Wayne suggested.

"Try anything you like," he said. "Nothing we have done has worked. I'm sorry that I can't help you," he added, a little choked up. "I'm a father myself, and I know what you must feel."

Back at Haddad's house that Sunday night, Wayne began to mix some evaporated milk with the barley water. David began to retain fluids. Patiently, diligently, we dropped liquid into his little mouth every hour, day and night. His recovery was not miraculous, it was not immediate. Gradually the loose wrinkles filled in with flesh, and his skin took on a healthy glow. As David gained weight and strength, a sparkle flashed through his big blue eyes, and his curly blond hair regained its sheen. By the middle of August he was definitely on the road to recovery.

Since the Russells would be returning to Middle East College when school started, the mission urged us to move immediately to the mountain village of Farhazier, where the climate would be healthier. Moses would stay in Shekka to maintain that base.

Wayne drove to Farhazier and found the house that God had designed to fit our needs. First of all, it was on the main road, centrally located, and easily accessible to everyone in the town. Although the front bordered the highway, a very generous sized, double staircase with a landing gave it a protective entrance. Double front doors led into a 12-foot wide hallway with a 15 x 15 foot room off each side of it. Ah! A large study for Wayne in the south room, and an evangelistic equipment and chair storage area in the north room. At the end of the entrance hall, another wider and longer hallway broke off to the left. This one was 16 x 34 feet—absolutely perfect for evangelistic meetings and church services. We could set up eighty-eight chairs in it and still have room for the pulpit at the north end. This area could be expanded still further by opening the double French doors into the private parlor, 15 x 16 feet, on one end, and the dining room, 9 x 16 feet, on the other end when needed. Off the hallway on the east were two large bedrooms, 15 x 15 feet each, and a 12 x 15 foot kitchen, plus the shower, toilet, and laundry area. Besides that, there were large covered verandas off the three sides of the house which did not face the road.

I took one look at this answer-to-our-prayer house and thought I was already in paradise. This was so ideal, such a perfect set-up for our purposes, that it had to have been built according to God's "specs". Here we could live and work comfortably, healthfully, and, I hoped, somewhat privately. When the "Man" had talked to me in Beit Meri, I could never have fathomed such a place awaited us. But He knew.

This was the first house to which Wayne had been directed when searching for our new location. The owners had started building the house on a grandiose scale, expecting an endless supply of money from the husband/father working in Uruguay. When his work came to an abrupt halt, their source of revenue was gone. They were forced to reside in the completed walk-out basement of the house until they could finish the inside of the first floor. When the mission saw this bonanza, they readily gave the family a year's rent in advance to complete the residence. Wayne and Moses moved our things up to Farhazir on August 15 (after Wayne sprayed with 100% DDT, of course). A week later, David was well enough to leave Beit Meri. What a day for rejoicing! We had survived a month of severe illness, were together again, and happier than ever to be missionaries in Lebanon.

Several of the "Man's" predictions had come true—David lived, he was recovering, and we had moved to Farhazier into an ideal home-evangelistic center. Now we were looking forward to the fulfillment of the other promises—to harvest the souls who accepted the gospel. It was not long in coming.

On October 15, our first four converts were baptized at the college. On December 31, Laurice and Widad Akar of Farhazier, Phillip of Shekka, and his friend were baptized. What with Edmond of Shekka, and Henry from Afesdik, this made a total of ten converts from North Lebanon in two years. For pioneer work in Arab Lands, this is a record for which only God can be praised. Besides this, more than 30 people attended the Sabbath services regularly, and interest was mushrooming all around us. This fulfilled the last prediction of the "Man" in Beit Meri.

Had God led us through the dark valley of a near-death experience to slow us down and help us learn to wait for Him to do the directing? Had we been so anxious to win souls that we ran ahead of the Lord's plans? We had been in a whirl of activity for months, sincerely believing we were doing God's work His way. And God blessed us, even as He pitied us.

Springtime in Farhazier: Midge, David, Ronnalee, and goats.

CHAPTER 17

GO TELL IT ON THE MOUNTAIN

We are accustomed to hearing about the hills of Palestine and the mountains of Lebanon. Both countries are hilly, and Lebanon has high mountains as well. Mount Hermon, more than 9,000 feet high, compares to the Mount of Olives at Jerusalem, about 3000 feet high. Both countries have nice coastal areas where all manner of semi-tropical foods can be grown the year around—citrus fruits, dates, bananas, and garden vegetables. A few miles inland, the elevation rises from one to two thousand feet where rolling or rugged hills are terraced to preserve the remaining soil. This is the fig, grape, berry, olive, cherry, plum, apricot, loquat, pomegranate, quince, persimmon, almond, walnut, and summer vegetable country. In the higher elevations of Lebanon the most delicious apples, peaches, and pears in the world are grown.

At about 6000 feet, one reaches the tree line level where the magnificent cedars of Lebanon, some of them millenniums old, still grow in all their splendor, spreading out their horizontal branches in a benediction to creation. In the summer, we often made the trek up the mile-high elevation to enjoy the perfumed atmosphere that surrounds the cedars; and in the winter, we played in the snow drifts beneath their snow-laden boughs. Both our children and our friends enjoyed skiing and sledding among the mammoth evergreens.

MIDGE IN LEBANON

Three thousand feet above and beyond the tree line were snow-covered mountain peaks topped with azure-blue skies. The quietude and grandeur of this place inspired a reverence within me. I felt that, if I could just reach through the blue canopy, I could touch God. South Dakota might have satisfied my childhood expectations, but here I knew awesomeness. Though this country is no longer a "land flowing with milk and honey," as God described it to Moses, yet, despite man's abuse and pollution, it remains productive and beautiful.

Beyond the Lebanon Mountains (ranging from 5000 to 9000+ feet) to the east, is the fruitful Bekaa Valley—the bread basket of Lebanon. East of that is the Anti-Lebanon Mountains (averaging 5,500 feet high). Their slopes descend into the Syrian plain and desert. We transversed all of this territory and explored the Crusader Castles, the Roman temple remains—especially Baalbek, the largest of them all—and watched the archaeologists dig at Tyre, Sidon, and Byblos. We visited many towns with houses centuries old, still in use and in good repair. We picnicked by gushing springs, swam in the warm water of Mediterranean bays, watched the oxen tread out the grain on the threshing floor in the same manner used in the Bible lands for thousands of years. THIS WAS LEBANON. This fascinating country and the friendly people latched onto our hearts. Never again would we be 100% Americans; we would forever be part Arab.

We lived in the rolling and rugged hill country where towns happened every two to three miles. Flames of gospel fires were igniting all over the mountains (as we called the hill country that surrounded us.) Needless to say, we were thrilled. It was just as the "Man" in Beit Meri had said. It interested us that many of the inquiries regarding our message were made by people in their teens and twenties. Sprinkled among them, of course, were the open-minded adults. We soon noted a definite mind-set pattern that had evidently developed among the Arabs through the centuries. Those ingrained with the traditional faiths of the Arab Lands—both Moslem and Eastern Christian believed that salvation was gained through something they could do. Evidently much stress had been placed upon their "doing" and "praying" rather a love relationship with God. Though many were not satisfied with their religion and enjoyed hearing the gospel message as taught by the Adventist church, yet they feared change more. Becoming an Adventist would mean giving up things they liked: gambling, tobacco, arak (the Lebanese equivalent of vodka), the family unity, and their friends.

We had been in Farhazier only a few weeks when we heard the most vicious rumor being circulated regarding us. Perhaps it was the best fabrication any priest ever invented to frighten the children in town from having anything to do with us. He told them the reason our baby was emaciated was that we were a cult who drank the blood of children in our rituals. And, since we had not been able to obtain blood from Lebanese children, we had used that of our own child. The idea was so repulsive to me that I wanted to pull out the hairs from his flowing beard, one by one. "No, Midge! Keep your cool!" I told myself. "God will clear up this rumor on His own. He doesn't need your help." So I bided my time—not altogether patiently.

During September, we had weekly meetings in our home, but only the Akars and Muellims families attended regularly. We sensed the prejudice and the keep-your-distance attitude, but we didn't know what we could do to change the people's minds. Almost no one believed the rumor, but, at the same time, the people were wary of us. Then, I believe, God used an unusual strategy to open the door of acceptance for us.

One day in early October, I was impressed to go downstairs to visit Afaaf, the daughter-in-law of our landlord. She was sitting in her living room, cradling little Ramon in her arms. Tears were streaming down her cheeks.

"Why the tears?" I asked solicitously.

"Ramon is burning up with fever, and I can't bring his temperature down," she sobbed. "Look, he's hardly conscious anymore. Oh God, what should I do?"

I listened to his short, raspy breaths and was immediately concerned. "Afaaf, I think he has pneumonia and needs penicillin or some medication immediately. Let Wayne take you to the doctor in Amuin."

"We don't have the money for the medicine or the doctor."

"Never mind that, Afaaf. If you don't get medical help immediately he might, ah, well, you know. We'll loan you the money for now if the doctor won't accept credit," I volunteered.

I don't know why I even suggested that we could pay for medication or the doctor. We were so poor in those days I made underwear for the children out of the good parts of Wayne's discards. But I was moved with compassion for the life of this child.

Afaaf was desperate and, therefore, easily convinced. She bundled up Ramon, and the next minute she and Wayne were on their way to Amuin. The doctor diagnosed Ramon as having a bad case of pneumonia and prescribed a course of antibiotics. Wayne bought the medicine for Afaaf; but now the problem was who would give the injections. In those days, penicillin was administered intramuscularly every three hours around the clock. Years earlier, Wayne had learned how to give injections and had most recently taken over the job of giving David vitamin injections twice weekly. Since there was no one else in town with this skill, Wayne conscientiously volunteered his services.

For the next five days and nights, Wayne boiled up his syringe and went down stairs to give little Ramon his shots every three hours. The baby soon recognized Wayne as Public Enemy Number One and cried whenever he entered the house. But Ramon got well, and this act of Christian service was noised abroad throughout the land. I have often suspected that the report of Wayne's faithful vigil improved with the passing of time. His position in the community rose eminently—somewhere between that of the Good Samaritan and St. Peter. Best of all, he was no longer connected with the Witch of Endor or Judas.

The next week a lady came to our door carrying her young son. "I know you helped Ramon, can you help my son too?" she pleaded, laying him down on one of the padded benches we had placed in the hallway. She pulled the blanket away from the leg of the semi-conscious child. What I saw sent chills through my body. My stomach revolted and I turned aside. This poor child had incurred a small cut on his foot. Then, oblivious to any danger, he played in the barnyard with the goats. Within three days, he developed septicemia. Now his leg was cold, swollen, and blackish colored all the way up to his hip. Obviously, the mother had come for our help much too late. That evening the little boy died. His death hurt us to the quick because we knew that the child would not have died if proper treatment would have been given to him sooner. From then on, anyone who came to our door with a medical need such as disinfecting a cut, treating a burn, needing water treatments or injections received our devoted attention.

MIDGE IN LEBANON

Thus, almost without our realizing what was happening, a first aid station for the town developed in our home. Some mornings we had many patients; other days there was no one needing our help. Since there was no doctor in the town, the people were very grateful for our knowledge of first aid. Prejudice melted like butter in the sun and our meetings were filled with people. Now the religious hierarchy was disturbed, and we sensed that perilous times for us were pending.

This all seemed so ludicrous. The Lebanese are a fantastic people—kind, hospitable, helpful, and the best of neighbors. There was almost nothing they or we wouldn't have done for one another. Religion wasn't an issue with us. We weren't forcing anyone to come to our meetings—people were free to come or go as they pleased. Why then should the religious leaders oppose us with violence? Perhaps they remembered that persecution had worked during the Dark Ages, and it was worth a try now. However, very few of the people collaborated with the clergy's efforts to harm us. They weren't even much concerned with excommunication.

Suspecting what lay ahead, Wayne began working on a permit to hold meetings in Farhazier. This time, however, he explored a new route.

First, he went to the office of the khaimakam, the district officer in charge of security. He talked briefly to Wayne in his office and then asked him to come see him in his home in Tripoli where he could speak more freely. The khaimakam claimed that whenever Wayne went to his office all the people milling around wanted to know what that foreigner wanted. Then the inquisitors would report everything to those who were opposing us. If the khaimakam attempted to help us, he would be in trouble with the bishop. He assured Wayne that he must get a permit if he hoped to continue his work.

Wayne explained that we were only preaching the gospel from the Bible and that we were helping the villagers with our first aid work. The officer broke into the conversation, "I know all that. The informers have already apprised me of that. I approve of what you are doing, but the law states that no public meetings can be held without an official, government permit. Every time you have a meeting, my telephone rings and the " (He held his open hand to the middle of his chest which was a gesture referring to the bishop with the long beard.) "asks me how come I allow you to meet without a permit. I'm being more than pressured over this. My job is in jeopardy."

Remembering our previous futile attempts to get meeting and school permits, Wayne didn't know where to turn. He asked the khaimakam for suggestions. "Well," the good man replied, "do you know anyone with some clout in Beirut?"

Wayne didn't know if Elder Keough had any political "clout" but that's where he went for advice. He suggested that Wayne talk to the President of the Higher Evangelical Council, an organization representing Protestant denominations in Lebanon. This council, among other things, acted as a clearing house for legal matters that were customarily handled by churches in Lebanon. Marriage and divorce certificates, for instance, had to be signed by the officiating minister of the denomination involved, then countersigned by the President of the Higher Evangelical Council. His signature was the only one recognized by the Lebanese government.

Wayne went to the President of the Council who listened attentively to our problem. He then wrote a paper that stated, "Wayne Olson is the Pastor of the Evangelical Church in Farhazier in North Lebanon."

But in Arabic, the difference between IN and the word AND when hand-written carelessly may not be easily distinguishable. Providentially, some copyist somewhere along the line wrote AND instead of IN. The completed copy now read, "Wayne Olson is the Pastor of the Evangelical Church in Farhazier AND North Lebanon." What a blessing this error proved to be in future years.

This document was then taken to the Minister of Justice who verified the signature of the President of the Evangelical Council and filed a copy of the paper. Next the document went to the Minister of Interior who also signed it and placed a copy in his File. In an unbelievable ten days the permit had made its rounds and was back in Wayne's hands!

Wayne and Farris Bishai, ministerial intern from Egypt, prayed before they took the document back to the khaimakam in Tripoli, hoping that he would now accept it as a bonified permit.

He read the paper, frowned, and said, "This is only from the Protestant Council. I need something from the government in Beirut." Wayne then pointed to the signatures of the Minister of Justice and the Minister of Interior. Then a smile spread over his face. "Excellent! Now write a letter to the Muhafaz stating that you have this permit." (Lebanon is divided into five states, each headed by an appointed, provincial governor called a Muhafaz)

"I'm not acquainted with the protocol," Wayne admitted. "Just what should I say in the letter?"

The khaimakam turned to Farris. "You know Arabic, don't you? Just write!"

"But how shall I state it in diplomatic language?" Farris questioned.

The khaimakam took a paper and pencil and wrote the letter in acceptable form. He then asked Farris to rewrite it in his own handwriting and had Wayne sign it.

"This is the way the system works," he explained. "Don't ask the Muhafaz for permission to hold meetings. If you do, he'll say no. TELL him you want to inform him that you have permission to hold meetings as indicated by the enclosed paper signed by the ministers of Justice and Interior. Then the Muhafaz will file a copy, sign it, and send it on to my office. I will keep the original on file. After that, no one can stop your meetings. If you need police protection, I can even provide that."

Little did we know the importance of that "piece of paper" at the time. During the next two years we would need to rely upon it as the basis for our right to police protection many, many times. That permit also gave us the liberty to work in ALL of North Lebanon, not just Farhazier as we had requested. God had led once more in a providential way to prepare for needs unknown to us.

Our home in Farhazier, where we held meetings after a 1952 Sabbath service. Men tried to throw four sticks of dynamite through the open double doors.

CHAPTER 18

"BLAST 'EM OUT"

"We'll blast you Adventists outa here yet," the village priest snarled as we met on the street one day. "Comin' around here pretending to be angels of mercy. HUH!"

I had a repartee on the tip of my tongue—"Better than being a person of destruction"—but I held my peace, forced a smile and walked on. We were soon to learn that his was not an idle threat. Since we had grown accustomed to such talk, we ignored it and went about our Father's business. So far, not one hair of our heads had been touched—close, maybe, but not quite. We continued to depend upon God's daily protection and not to worry about the morrow. I never could have explained the contentment I experienced during those years in North Lebanon. Even amidst the storms of opposition, I enjoyed great peace of mind. Each day I felt God was walking right beside me, holding my hand.

With the official permit, spoken of in the previous chapter, we continued the meetings in our home in Farhazier. Now, however, the hall was packed. We had proved our friendship with our first aid service. The village people loved and trusted us as we did them. I felt very secure in Farhazier until...

One night I stood at the doorway of our home, as usual, welcoming the people as they came to the meeting. I lingered in the doorway even after Wayne began his sermon. The spring evening was warm and pleasant, and I was enjoying the quiet that comes to a small town at the end of a day. Suddenly my attention was drawn to a group of men coming up the street. Since the main road was only two feet from our front steps, I was used to traffic coming and going. In the evenings, I often stood out on our landing and visited with the people as they passed by on their evening promenade. But the strolling time was over now. As I observed more closely, there seemed to be something suspicious about the men approaching our house. I had a premonition that we were their target. I stepped back into the shadows beside the door to observe them. As they came into view, I recognized the village priest, two monks, and a couple of ruffians. Each of the monks carried two whitish sticks. What was it? I couldn't be certain. They stopped just 10 feet from our house and faced our front door. Then the ruffians lit the sticks, and the monks hurled them at our open door. I ducked, knowing then that it was dynamite. Hadn't the priest promised to "blast us"? I closed my eyes, expecting to be blown away. Seconds later I heard the explosion off to the side of our house. I finally got the courage to look out the door. People came running from all over the village and were milling about in the street. "What happened?" they yelled.

The men who had come to "blast us" were in shock. One monk kept muttering, "But I aimed them right at the front door. How could the dynamite have gone astray—turning to the right at the door, and then making a left turn at the corner of the house. Where did it land?"

"I don't know," mumbled the others who was obviously just as confused.

"I'll tell you where it landed," the owner of our house shouted angrily from the terrace below. "In the empty

"BLAST 'EM OUT"

cistern off the corner of my house. It nearly broke our windows, and it scared my donkey out of the country."

Mr. Akar, the friend who had invited us to Farhazier, arrived at the scene. "Are you people CRAZY?" he demanded of the priest and his cronies. "Don't you realize you could have killed people? My wife and six children are in there. So are 50 or more of my other friends. Will you kill that many people just to get rid of the Adventists?" he spit out the words contemptuously. "You should be prosecuted for this insane act!"

Everyone on the street concurred. Then the crowd became angry and restless. Quickly the priest and his crowd disappeared into the shadows before someone could harm them.

In the seclusion of our huge inside hallway surrounded by large rooms which cushioned the sound, our meeting went on completely undisturbed. Hardly anyone had heard the explosion. What peace have those who serve the Lord!

After the dynamite fiasco, we knew the priest and his associates would have to lay low for a few months. The people had seen the lengths to which a religious leader would go to keep them from studying the Bible, and they were angered by his attempt to thwart their liberty. If anyone tried to stop our meetings now the people would rise up against them. Our enemies had unwittingly helped our cause. I wondered if God didn't have a good laugh over the way He had thwarted Satan's plans. I know we did.

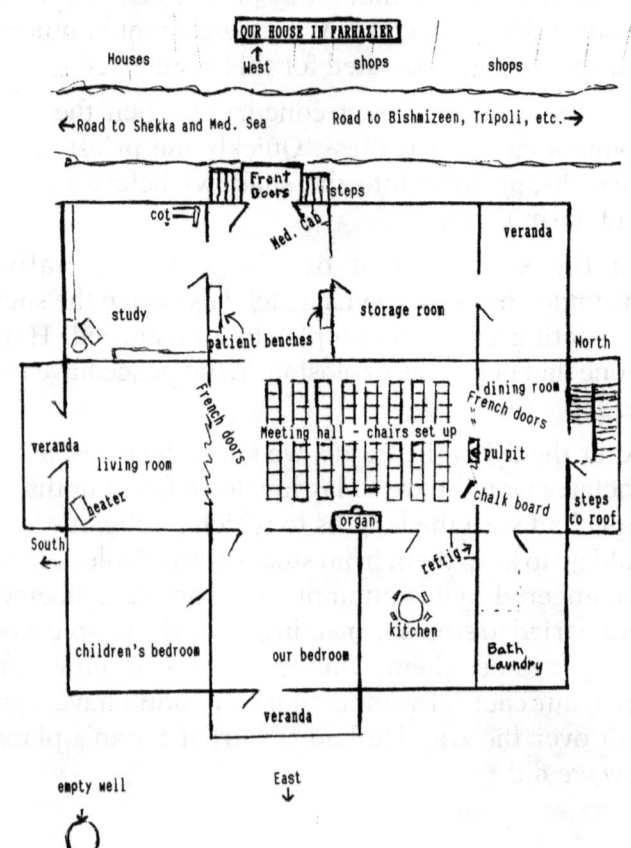

CHAPTER 19

GIVE US THIS DAY OUR DAILY BREAD AND TIME TO EAT IT

"...then, because so many people were coming and going, they did not even have a chance to eat." Mark 6:31 (NIV) It happened to Jesus' disciples, and now we had reached that point in our work too. It seemed there was always someone at our door needing help. Our house was the evangelistic center, church, and mission headquarters in North Lebanon, and the village first aid station. It had become difficult for us to eat a meal or to do any household chores without being interrupted. That year we had only one night at home alone with the family—and that was because the weather threatened another Noah-size deluge.

We, however, considered this contact with the people and the demand for Bible studies and cottage meetings a special blessing. This was why we were here! The rapidly expanding interest was quite amazing considering the fact that we had been in North Lebanon for only two years. Previous to our coming, Adventists had been unknown in the north half of Lebanon. Already we were working in five villages, and the cities of Shekka and Tripoli.

When we first moved to the north, other Protestants warned us that it was difficult to arouse interest in the gospel message in the mountain villages. Furthermore, it was dangerous—their last three village ministers had been pushed over a 1200 foot cliff to their death. By now, we believed them. We too would have been dead had not God delivered us.

We would never have been able to fulfill the visitation requests had it not been for the foresight of the mission in sending us good help. Michael Kebbas worked in the Rutga area, Moses Ghazal in Shekka and Ras Maska, Farris Bishi in Farhazier, Bishmizeen, and Afesdik, while Wayne ran himself ragged trying to touch base with all the interests. Since I was the only woman on the evangelistic team, I averaged at least two visits/studies per day in the homes of interested ladies. Besides that, I helped with the first aid, played my accordion at cottage meetings, held branch Sabbath Schools, planned recreation in our home every Saturday night, and entertained guests. Though all of us suffered from fatigue, it was a good sort of tiredness. We were so thrilled with our work we didn't even care if we had no time to rest or eat.

The mission officers gave us complete freedom to preach the gospel in North Lebanon wherever the Holy Spirit indicated. The mission leaders approved of what we were doing because it was working. We wished we had had more guidance, but none of them had been involved in the pioneering type of work we were doing except Elder George Keough. He advised, "Don't light more fires than you can feed." But, in our zeal, we did.

The one grief of my life was David's health. Every third Friday he got another case of vomiting and diarrhea. The doctor would then put him on sulfa for a week, and David would be all right for the next two weeks. Then the cycle would repeat itself again. This recurring problem became a "thorn in my flesh."

People from out of town came for the Sabbath services in Farhazier and then stayed for the afternoon M.V. meetings and evening recreation. This meant that I needed to provide Sabbath dinners and suppers for 20

GIVE US THIS DAY OUR DAILY BREAD AND TIME TO EAT IT

or more extra people. This was not a burden—just Arab hospitality. We always ate with the Lebanese when we were in their vicinity. Much as I enjoyed all the facets of our work, yet everything I did required time—something I was running short on.

Although we were always short of money, we hired a girl to run countless errands, set up and take down the chairs for the meetings, and help with the daily cleaning. It seemed that the wide hallways were constantly dirty. People came off the muddy side streets, tramping dirt into the house all day long. The $10 we paid her was not much, but it was a 15th of our salary. Therefore, we asked the mission to pay her wages. I was disappointed that the mission president would not even bring our request to the committee. I fumed to myself, "How can the mission president pay the office secretaries for their work and not even give me a pittance for mine? Isn't soul-winning work as important as office work? We are out here on the front line risking life and limb doing evangelistic work."

We knew that minister's wives weren't paid for doing Bible work, and we weren't asking for an exception to that policy. We only wanted reimbursement for the janitorial work done in our home—evangelistic center and first aid clinic. If anyone could have read my secret thoughts he would have known that God had not perfected sainthood in me yet. I let what seemed like an inequality to me fester within me until it began to affect my Christian experience. Then God helped me get back on track. I knew the mission president would not resolve the issue, so I did. I forgave the president, and God forgave me. I learned that although things sometimes seem inequitable, God has a way of making them come out right.

MIDGE IN LEBANON

The mission president finally gave us a budget of three dollars a month to buy our first aid supplies. Of course, that small amount never covered our personal expenditures. But we couldn't stop this work, either. The people depended upon our help, and this medical work broke down prejudice.

Then a General Conference officer wrote a classic article in the REVIEW about our mini-medical clinic and its influence. A doctor in California read the story, and God impressed him to help. From then on, the doctor kept us supplied with bandages and medicines. This saved us personally about $15 per month. That was a lot of money in those days.

The most useful medication the doctor sent was a three-pound jar of burn ointment. It had some ingredient in it that minimized the pain of burns. In the winter, many children got burned by falling into the open charcoal fire pots used for heating the homes. One little toddler fell across the fire pot and burned his stomach. The mother rushed the screaming child to us. We spread a thick layer of the ointment onto a cloth, placed it over his tummy, and it relieved his pain almost immediately. There were all kinds of facial, hand and leg burns as well. It was surprising how quickly the medicine healed the burns leaving almost no scars. Of course, it turned my stomach when Wayne peeled off the dead skin or flesh, but I learned how to survive that—I left the room.

One Monday morning I was washing clothes when a man rushed into the house without even knocking. "Olsons, come quickly, QUICKLY. The priest's* six-year old granddaughter was playing with a stick in the charcoal fire, and a spark ignited her dress. She got scared and ran outside; the wind fanned the flames into an inferno. She is burned from head to foot and is beside

GIVE US THIS DAY OUR DAILY BREAD AND TIME TO EAT IT

herself with pain. I know the priest tried to kill you, but have pity on this child, if you can," he begged.

I turned off the washer immediately, grabbed the burn ointment, rags, and a sheet. I pushed the messenger out the door, and together we ran to the priest's home. "Of course, I'll try to help her," I explained to the man as we raced along, slipping and sliding down the muddy street. "I would gladly help the priest himself. I'm offended that you would think otherwise. Christians don't hold grudges."

The child was laying on the cold tile floor, shaking and groaning. Her clothes had been burned off. Even her beautiful little face was a mass of seared flesh, and her lovely brown curls were singed crisp. She had suffered first and second degree burns over most of her body. I wanted to cry—I knew she would never live. I smeared the ointment onto the sheet and wrapped her in it. The medication relieved some of her pain, and she relaxed a little. Then I had someone call Wayne from the neighboring village where he had gone for a Bible study. A half hour later Wayne and her father loaded the little girl into our Ford and headed for the hospital in Amuin. The doctor knew immediately that he could not save her. He could hardly find a place on her body where he could give her a morphine shot. She died that night, and we attended her funeral the next day. In the Middle East, funerals are held within 24 hours of death since there is no embalming.

"See how pure the religion of the Adventists is! They love their enemies and do good to those who hate them," the villagers said remembering the dynamite fiasco. Truthfully, I had not even given a thought to witnessing when I rushed to the side of the suffering child. I responded because God's compassion is inherent in His followers. It didn't matter who she or her relatives were.

MIDGE IN LEBANON

We expressed our sympathy to the family who were grateful that, at least, the burn medication had relieved some of the child's suffering. Even the old priest, with tears in his eyes, shook our hands. He couldn't speak beyond the lump in his throat. Maybe he was suffering guilt or seeking forgiveness. It didn't really matter; we had become one in spirit through the human grieving process. All barriers between us were now gone.

"May God comfort you. We love you," I said through my tears as I patted his arm. It was true. I had honestly come to love the old man and his family. He had only tried to get rid of us because he thought it was best for the people.

We treated snake, bee, and scorpion bites, burns, cuts, and infections. Wayne gave hundreds of injections. We even placed a cot in his study where the patients could lie down while Wayne injected their hips. The ladies insisted that I drape a sheet modestly around their hips in such a way that only the necessary flesh for the injection was exposed. None of them wanted Pastor Olson to "see their body."

The most time consuming of our clinical work was the water treatments. However, we enjoyed chatting with the patient as we applied the hot and cold compresses, and the treatments almost always cured the stubborn infections.

One particularly interesting case was that of the butcher who had his meat shop next door to our house. Meat was sold in the village every Wednesday and Sunday mornings. The fact that we encouraged vegetarianism, antagonized the butcher. He treated us coolly and spoke disparagingly about us.

One Sunday morning a villager walked past his shop to purchase meat from his competitor a half block down the street. The butcher had been eating raw meat dipped

GIVE US THIS DAY OUR DAILY BREAD AND TIME TO EAT IT

in arak—a vodkalike beverage. This combination tends to benumb one's inhibitions and common sense.

"Stop, Saleem," he yelled angrily at the villager. "Buy your meat from me."

"I'll buy my meat where I want. You just stay out of my business," Saleem responded contemptuously. Saleem wasn't in a good mood, either.

"Don't you talk like that to me, you, you dog. You son of a whore," growled the butcher as he dashed into the street to attack Saleem.

The men got into physical combat. It took seven other men to separate them. When it was all over, Saleem's chin was bleeding where the butcher bit him, and the butcher lost half of his Hitler-like mustache to the teeth of Salcem. The peace makers scolded the two combatants, trying to make them see the stupidity of their actions.

After the two calmed down, they came to our house for treatment. I made the butcher sit on one bench and Saleem on the other bench facing him. Then, before I treated them, I gave them a lecture that could have equaled one of Carrie Nation's remonstrances impugning liquor. When they appeared reasonably penitent, I disinfected Saleem's gashes, bandaged them, and dismissed him. Then I turned to the butcher. The half of the mustache torn loose from his upper lip was dangling by only a thin piece of skin. I cringed as I cut it off. The flesh above his upper lip that had once supported half of the proud butcher's mustache, was now pitifully mutilated. I waited until the wound quit bleeding. Then I disinfected it as best I could, smeared on some carbolic salve, and advised him to see a doctor. He left but was too ashamed to go to a doctor. He insisted that "Doctora Olson" had done a good enough job. His wound finally healed but it left a scar. That was the end of the butcher's mustache, because half a mustache is really no mustache at all. The good result of this experience was that we gained two more friends, and a chuckle.

Engagements, weddings, child births, and funerals were occasions that we also needed to wedge into our busy schedule.

Another important item on our daily agenda was to perfect our Arabic. Farris came to the house each day to teach classical Arabic to Wayne. They read, wrote, and talked the sophisticated version. I discovered a novel, less painful way of mastering the colloquial language. I sat with the women at the "furn", the social center for the village ladies. My curiosity drove me to learn Arabic fast so I could enjoy my female companions and get in on the village gossip.

The furn is a large, one-room bakery. Along the middle of one side is a six-foot diameter, dome-shaped brick oven. Since none of the homes in those days had ovens, this is where the women came to bake their bread. So the furn was very essential to the villager's life. I was the only woman in town who owned a butane stove with an oven. The other ladies cooked their food over one-burner primus stoves.

Early each morning the owner of the furn, Mrs. Muellim, stoked up the fire by burning straw and wood in the center of the oven. When the bricks were properly heated, she swept the glowing ashes around the edges of the oven to hold the heat.

Then she was ready to bake the bread for her customers. The village women, whose turn it was to bake bread that day, brought their dough to the furn at the appointed times. They sat on low stools facing a two-foot wide counter and rolled out their pita bread. When Mrs. Muellim placed her flat, fan-shaped paddle in front of a customer, the lady threw her rolled-out loaf onto it, and

GIVE US THIS DAY OUR DAILY BREAD AND TIME TO EAT IT

the baker slipped it onto the hot bricks of the oven. I never ceased to marvel at the efficiency of the baker as she moved around the circle with her paddle, filling the oven with many loaves, and then slipping the right loaf back to the owner precisely when the product was perfected. Thus Mrs. Muellim serviced a half dozen customers at once.

I always bought bread from the women at the furn because I certainly didn't have time to make the dough, roll it out, and bake it. Besides, I was too busy trying to learn Arabic and filling my little book with colloquial expressions. I acted out all kinds of ridiculous motions to get verbs; I pointed at objects to learn nouns. The ladies loved my visits and clapped when I entered the furn—I guess I provided entertainment for them. The women laughed good-naturedly at my mistakes and made me repeat a phrase until I could say it just like they did. When I succeeded they called me a Lebanese, a compliment I treasured. They were very pleased with their success in teaching me Arabic. They bragged, "Mrs. Olson talks more like a Lebanese than her husband even though he can read and write the language."

Besides getting to feel a part of my community, I gathered enough gossip at the furn to entertain Wayne all during supper.

Meanwhile, David and Ronnie were learning Arabic too. Ronnie played with Germana, a little girl her age that lived down the block, and David shared his toys with Ramon, the neighbor's son. (Ramon was the child who Wayne had injected with penicillin when we first arrived in Farhazier.) Before we knew it, Arabic became the language of our home.

We had planned a baptism for the last Sabbath of the year with the Akar girls as two of the candidates. On

MIDGE IN LEBANON

Friday morning, Farris hurried to our house with the disappointing news that their father now refused to allow them to take this rite. "WHY?" we wondered. Akars were the best of friends and we ate with them frequently. They had brought us to this area. They had always supported our work. The father had not objected to his oldest son, Alfred, being baptized. What could be the problem now?

Farris and Wayne went to the Akars to talk with the father. They learned that the real objection was coming from Uncle Haleem, who had also been a special friend to us. Wayne and Farris consulted with him. Haleem argued, "The girls are beautiful, intelligent, and ready for college. Professional men will ask their hand in marriage. But if they become Adventists, who will want them? At this point they have a bright future ahead of them. They will attract men of wealth and prominence and live a comfortable life."

"And then?" Wayne asked pointedly. "Is this life all there is to be for the girls? Haleem, just imagine that the Lord came and took you to heaven where you enjoy a 1000-year vacation. Then the Holy City, New Jerusalem, descends back to earth and you are inside looking out. Suddenly you see Laurice and Widad standing outside the wall with Satan and his people. You turn to the Lord in astonishment and ask why those two good girls are out there. And the Lord answers, 'When they wanted to give their hearts to the Lord fully, you, Haleem, objected. You wanted them to have a comfortable earthly life, which they have had. However, the pressures brought upon them by their growing families and in-laws discouraged them, and they gave up trying to serve the Lord. You know, Haleem, that I have to keep heaven safe for those who are willing to make a covenant with me—and sometimes this required

GIVE US THIS DAY OUR DAILY BREAD AND TIME TO EAT IT

sacrifice. So now the girls will have to be eternally destroyed with the others out there."'

Haleem turned pale. "Mr. Olson, you scare me. I would rather see the girls saved eternally. Go ahead and baptize them tomorrow, and we'll just trust their future to God."

December 31, Widad and Laurice were baptized along with Phillip and Sam.

The work was going well in Afesdik too. Every Sunday morning Farris, Wayne and I went to the Melkie home for services. Mr. Melkie's oldest son, Henry, was a sophomore at Middle East College and had already been baptized. Hyatt and Edmund Melkie were still at home attending Bishmizeen High School. They were avid Bible students who enjoyed sharing the good news with their classmates.

One day in English class Hyatt was asked to write a sentence on the chalkboard. Anxious to appropriate every opportunity to witness she wrote, "The seventh-day is the Sabbath; but some people think Sunday is the holy day."

The teacher was incensed. "That is wrong, WRONG!" he shouted.

"Oh. Is there something wrong with my grammar?" Hyatt asked coyly.

"The grammar is right, but the, aaah, idea is HERESY," he responded angrily. "Don't you go broadcasting the strange notions of the Adventists here!"

"That's what the Bible teaches," Hyatt said politely as she took her seat. The message was not lost on her classmates. Students from Bishmizeen now started attending our Sunday evening meetings in Farhazier.

In April, the Nabtis opened their home and we began cottage meetings in Bishmizeen. We knew we needed to do this to keep the interest of the people alive, but fitting an evening time slot into our already packed schedule was difficult. Besides the meeting, there would be the home visitations to make. I had reached my limit, so I dropped out and left the men to handle it.

Busy as we were, our work was made easier by the fact that we had had no persecution to speak of in four months. Where were our enemies? I knew the devil hadn't died. We had learned to expect hostility whenever we entered a new town with our message, but, surprisingly, we had none in either Afesdik or Bishmizeen. Perhaps, after the dynamite fiasco, the monks were laying low for fear of the people, and the priest in Farhazier had been reconciled to sharing his town with the Adventists. We never knew when or where or how the enemy would strike next. Even if this peace didn't last, it was nice to have a respite.

I don't know how Wayne and the interns managed those stressful days when we were too busy to eat our daily bread, but I knew how to handle mine. Whenever the daily cares became overwhelming, I retired to Mrs. Muellim's furn where everyone was my friend. There I could relax with the ladies, AND take time to enjoy eating fresh-from-the-oven pita bread.

*In some denominations, priests marry and have families.

CHAPTER 20

THE STEP TO SUCCESS

June 17 we had our largest baptism to date. We hired a bus to carry those who wished to witness the solemn rite down to Jonah's Bay (so called because tradition says this might have been the place where the whale coughed up Jonah.) Besides our local people, some of the students and teachers came from Middle East College. Many of the mission workers also came from Beirut to see the baptism of Nada, Elias, and Alice Muellim, Hyatt and Edmund Melkie, Nabi Akar, and Yusif and Riad Lemik. It was a happy, sacred occasion even though the waves played havoc with the baptismal robes.

We returned to Farhazier rejoicing, had sundown worship together at our house, ate a snack, and enjoyed an evening social with the youth. At ten o'clock everyone went home except the Muellim children. They dreaded facing their older brother Khalil who had become the "boss" in the family after their father was blinded in an explosion at the cement factory. Khalil had specifically told his siblings that they should not be baptized, and they had done it anyway. Wayne walked home with Alice, Nada, and Elias to face Khalil.

When they entered the house, Khalil was livid with anger. Wayne called him outside and tried to reason with him, but Khalil would not listen.

Wayne left then, knowing the tension within the home was like stretched rubber bands. Khalil claimed he was tired from working all day. He turned off the lights and forbade anyone to turn them on again. Elias, Nada, and Alice wanted to study their Sabbath School lesson, so they took their Bibles and quarterlies and went out under the street light. When they went back to the house, Khalil had locked the door and refused to let them in. Elias went to a field to sleep, but the girls knocked on our door.

"Please, Mrs. Olson, may we stay with you tonight?" Nada asked.

"Of course," I said inviting them in. "May I ask what has happened?"

"Sure. Khalil locked us out of the house," Alice said simply. "He is very angry because we were baptized."

"But why is Khalil antagonistic now?" I asked. "He comes to most of our meetings himself."

"That is true," Alice agreed. "He believes the Adventists teach the truth, but he doesn't have the faith to obey it. We do owe a lot to Khalil. He has supported our family for five years. He can't even afford to get married because he has to spend all his money on us."

"I know, but that doesn't give him the right to rule your lives," I argued.

"Mrs. Olson, you don't understand," Nada added, patiently trying to explain Middle East psychology. "The father in an Arab home is in charge of all the family affairs. When our father was blinded Khalil assumed the father role. He gave up his education and went to work painting houses to earn a living for the family. He wants for us what he sacrificed—an education and a professional job. He thinks that now we will get neither. No one will hire us since we won't work on Sabbath, and we can't finish our education since he doesn't have the money to pay our full tuition in the Bishmizeen High

THE STEP TO SUCCESS

School. In previous years, the school granted us scholarships because of father's disability. Khalil says they won't do that next year since the faculty doesn't like Adventists. He's probably right. Well, I don't care; I feel so wonderfully close to my friend Jesus. I wouldn't exchange my peace of mind for any diploma or job in the world. I'm willing to trust my future to God."

I looked at the girls. They knew what it meant to sacrifice for Christ, yet they were perfectly content. Nothing could dim their faith. They were willing to loose their education, future, and Khalil's favor to serve Jesus.

I opened up the davenport and made a bed for them. Then we prayed together and kissed each other goodnight.

Four days went by and still Khalil did not invite the three back home. During the daytime they would sneak home and get some clothes. Finally the parents intervened, and Alice, Nada, and Elias returned home to an uneasy peace. At first Khalil refused to talk to his siblings at all, but "chatterbox" Nada finally broke his silence. Khalil forgave them because he really did love them. He was sorry they had given up the possibility of getting their high school diplomas and good jobs, but they would have to live with the consequences.

* * * * * *

At the time, none of us knew the future God had planned for the three "worthies", but it was good. Their decision to be baptized was actually their step to success. Alice got work as a seamstress. Nada and Elias did get scholarships for their senior year. What is more, a year down the road, God inspired a person in America to send us a check to help "some worthy students go to Middle East College." We didn't have a hard time deciding for whom God had targeted that check. Nada and Elias went to MEC for their college education. Besides the money from America, they both worked hard to earn as much of their tuition as possible.

After leaving Middle East College, Elias got a job with the American Embassy in Beirut where he has worked more than 30 years. Because of his honesty and faithfulness, he has received many promotions with an increase in salary. Financially, Elias was well able to support his parents in their old age. Nada became a Bible worker and teacher. She married John Hancock, an Adventist marine she met in Lebanon, and came to America. They have two sons, John and Raymond, who graduated from Loma Linda University. God rewarded the Muellim children with success in this life, and they look forward to an even better life in the world to come.

The hard-working and loving brother Khalil and younger brother Nadeem are enjoying their life in America.

CHAPTER 21

THE EXPLOSION ???!!!

It was summer and too hot to keep the front door closed during the day. I liked an open door policy for the convenience of our first aid patients but was getting tired of the flies coming in our front door as if the same policy applied to them too. David, now one and a half years old, also liked the open door—only he went the opposite direction of the flies. Every time he got a chance, he sneaked out the front door and onto the very busy street. In Fahazier this was especially hazardous since there were no sidewalks and the buildings hugged the road. I usually retrieved the boy in one of the roadside cafes feasting on cookies and pop; but the danger of his being on the street at all worried me. I feared that one day a car would hit him. We had to do something to curtail David's innocent attempts at suicide and to discourage the flies.

Wayne studied the situation. "I think I have the solution. I'll buy screen in Beirut and get the landlord's permission to put it on our doors and windows. Even though houses here aren't built for screens, I know how I can fasten them on this type of door. It will keep David in and the flies out."

"It would also keep sticks of dynamite or firecrackers out, if anyone was inclined to make such an attempt again," I observed. I still jumped at any explosive sound—even when a car backfired.

MIDGE IN LEBANON

June 23, 1950 Wayne entertained curious onlookers by putting screens on our windows, but the most interesting phase of the work was making the screen doors. Since Wayne could not find the right size lumber, he used 2 x 3 inch boards to make the frames. The right door of the front double doors he fastened more or less permanently shut with pins and then braced it in the middle with a thick board. On the other side he made a sturdy, hinged screen door. Since the doors were so wide, we needed only one screen door to open. He fastened a hook high on the frame so the children couldn't reach it. Now we were set for summer.

We faced a busy summer; we had scheduled a full-fledged evangelistic effort for Bishmizeen. We had had no opposition in Farhazier since we had attempted to save the life of the priest's granddaughter. Nothing of consequence had transpired in Afesdik or Bishmizeen, either.

Just when we thought we had settled into a peaceful coexistence with the ruling Christian church of the valley, our lives were threatened again. It came unexpectedly and fiercely from the greatest power figure within that church.

An urgent message was sent to the people of Farhazier, demanding that they go to the church yard on Sunday morning. The Bishop himself would come from Tripoli to address them. A visit from the Bishop was a rare treat, so the church yard was packed with people as he drove up in his limousine. The Bishop, arrayed in his finest robes and carrying his staff, stepped from the car and mounted the steps. His body guards stood on either side of him, gazing down disdainfully at the people. The Bishop surveyed the hushed audience who waited reverently to hear his message. At last he chose to begin. "Hear ye, O my people of Farhazier. In the past, you

THE EXPLOSION ???!!!

have been brave, honorable people, respected by God and by me; but now this village stinks. You have allowed the disease of Adventism to incubate among you. You have allowed them to hold meetings right in the center of your village. As you pass the Advent house, you are lured in to hear them like Eve listening to the serpent. Why have you permitted them to stay here? It is your fault that they have spread their cancer to the surrounding towns of Afesdik and Bishmizeen. Shame on you!"

The Bishop harangued the people for half an hour, calling them dogs, cowards etc. At last he challenged them, "Throw out the Adventists tonight! Break into their meeting, carry out the traitors, assault Olson and his scoundrels. Let someone do his duty to God and for the church..."

"Just a minute!" an angry voice shouted from the edge of the crowd. "Who do you think you are coming here telling us what we should do? The Adventists are good, peace-loving people. They give us help with no remuneration. You black crows with beards (insultingly referring to the black, flowing robes worn by the bearded priests) come around with both hands open, taking more money from us all the time."

The voice was that of Joseph, our landlord's grown son. The crowd was stunned at Joseph's audacity. As he pressed his way toward the Bishop, the crowd separated like the Red Sea giving him passage. Seething with anger, Joseph leaped onto the platform and shook his leaded stick in the Bishop's face. "The Adventists meet in my house. Don't tell me I can't pray with them in my own house. Don't ever attempt to come into my house and stop them. If you or your henchmen do, your bloody heads will roll down the front steps!" With this final threat, Joseph jumped off the platform and went home.

MIDGE IN LEBANON

Joseph had broken the spell of the Bishop's oratory. A riot nearly broke out in the church yard as some aligned themselves with Joseph and us, and some supported the Bishop. As the tide seemed to be turning in our favor, the Bishop and his entourage decided they should get out of town, immediately! Gradually the rest of the crowd dispersed and went home.

Presently people swarmed into our house to inform us of what had transpired in the church yard. They were very concerned for our lives. "Don't have any meeting tonight, Mr. Olson," they begged. "There are a few hotheads in town that don't like you because you talk against gambling, drinking, cheating, and womanizing. Your sermons bother their consciences. If these men start drinking tonight, they may make an attempt on your life to satisfy the hierarchy. Please don't hang out your meeting sign."

Wayne, being a stubborn Swede with a trust in God, would not be persuaded. He hung out the chalkboard sign advertising the subject on which he would speak that Sunday night, anyway. As usual, the people could read the advertisement as they walked home from church. He had done it every Sunday for six months and he would continue to do so now. Some of us thought the better part of wisdom was to cancel the next two Sunday night meetings. In two weeks we would have to stop them anyway since we would begin the effort in Bishmizeen then. But Wayne would not be intimidated by threats.

It was a tense Sunday in Farhazier. Little huddles of men secretly discussed the pros and cons of the Bishop's suggestions. Before nightfall, it was rumored that someone planned to cut off the electricity from our house after the meeting began, then rush up to the front of the meeting hall, grab Wayne, kill him, and anyone

THE EXPLOSION ???!!!

who got in their way. We were surprised that anyone dared come to our meeting that night, but they did.

Wayne customarily drove to Bishmizeen and picked up the ten to fourteen young people who wished to hear the Sunday night sermons in Farhazier. Wayne packed them in the Ford—one passenger on each of the front fenders, three in the front seat with him, five or six in the back seat sitting double, and three in the open trunk. If there were more, Wayne had to make an extra trip. Since gas was expensive, we tried to limit our trips whenever possible. (The savings in gas, however, was off-set by the money spent to replace broken springs!)

Amazingly, the people from Bishmizeen had already heard that there may be trouble in our house that night, but they came anyway. Among them were several young men who had never been there before and one of the area communist leaders. The communist was big—over six feet tall and weighed close to 250 pounds. He swaggered in the door and came up to me, "I've heard they're gonna kill your husband tonight. But don't worry. I'll take care of 'em. I brought my hunting knife." He grinned fiendishly.

I drew back and looked at his weapon, hoping that he really was on our side. I became very distrustful of him and wondered if he was relegated to be the hit man. Was his talk of "protection" just a ploy to disarm me? I wished he would leave but certainly didn't have the courage to suggest it.

"I'm not afraid of anyone or anything," the bully boasted. "I stop 'em DEAD in their tracks." He cut the air with his knife to emphasis his point. I gulped; my heart skipped ten beats. "I came along specifically to protect Mr. Olson," he continued. "When I'm around no one dares to start trouble unless I say so! Know what I mean?" he whispered too close to my face.

MIDGE IN LEBANON

I nodded obediently, quite anxious not to arouse his animal instincts. Satisfied that he had convinced me of his absolute control of any situation, he turned and strutted to the front row. He took the chair directly in front of the podium.

Our friends from Bishmizeen along with those from Farhazier almost filled our meeting hall (house) that Sunday night—perhaps 75 people in all. I noticed, however, that we all were pretty edgy. When a car backfired, we jumped and looked around us. Moses tried to calm his fears by singing exceptionally loud during the song service, but no one followed his example. Never before had the song service been so deficient in spirit. I pulled out all the stops on the pump organ hoping it would drown out the thumping sound of my heart. Everyone fidgeted nervously, obviously primed for trouble.

June 25, 1950 was a warm night. We opened the newly-screened windows and let the air circulate through both sides of our screened, double doors. Yet the people were sweltering. Since Wayne was still in his office praying, I asked Mike Nabti to help me. I continued to play the organ as I explained to Mike, "Get the circular fan in the washroom and plug it into the transformer in the kitchen. Set it in the center of the room between the rows of girls."

I guess Mike only heard part of what I said. He plugged the 110 volt fan directly into the 220-volt wall outlet instead of the transformer. What happened in the next few minutes added an incredible chapter to the history of Farhazier. With the electrical current doubled, the fan blades whirred and turned like fury. Before I could get Mike to unplug it, smoke arose from the fan, encircling the girls. In seconds, the motor burned out shorting the wires, blowing the fuse, and

THE EXPLOSION ???!!!

leaving the whole house in darkness. The girls saw and smelled the smoke just as the lights went out. They assumed that a grenade had been planted under them, and that they would be soon be blown into eternity. Blood-curdling screams rent the air and set off a human stampede that was without precedence. The whole crowd assumed that the rumored plot was being enacted as planned. The lights had gone out in the Adventist's house; next, there would be a murder. No one wanted to be a part of that action. Total bedlam ensued—people ran in all directions, screaming, bumping into one another, and knocking over chairs in an effort to escape the explosion and/or the assassin.

At the precise moment that the lights went out, Wayne stepped out of the room where he had been praying into the entrance hallway. He had to vault back into the doorway to keep from being trampled. He saw the first person headed for the screen door—it was the big, brave communist leader! Our "protector" was in such a hurry to flee that he crashed through the stationary screen of the front doors. He hit the thick cross piece of wood so hard that it splintered into pieces and tore out the permanent screen with it. Then, like Samson carrying off the gates of Gaza, our commie carried off the "expermanent" screened half of our front door into the street and dropped it as he disappeared in a cloud of dust. So much for his help!

The second person out the front door was Jamili, only she went through the hinged screen door. She too had been sitting near the front of the hall. How those two, the Commie and Jamili, could possibly have gotten past 60 other people to reach the front door first has been a wonderment to all of us. This was especially amazing for Jamili. She was a beautiful, middle-aged lady, whose ample figure testified to the excellent cuisine she provided with her gourmet cooking. She hadn't seen any of her bones in years. And, weighing in at about 235 lbs., Jamili hadn't moved fast in 20 years, either. Yet she was the second person out the door!

Jamili didn't stop when she got outside, either. She headed for the protection of her house at the top of the hill. Half way up she met the wife of the blind man, Mrs. Muellim, who was on her way to our meetings. She had been detained by some work she had to do in their bakery.

"Jamili! " Mrs. Muellim cried, grabbing her arm, "Why are you rushing like this? Remember your blood pressure? You know the doctor has strictly forbidden you to exercise vigorously."

Jamili wrenched her arm free from Mrs. Muellim's grasp. "Don't stop me now!" she puffed, her eyes bulging in their sockets and her flushed face dripping with perspiration. "I'm fleeing from the explosion at Olsons' house. I, only I, escaped!" Then Jamili raced on up the hill, leaving Mrs. Muellim in a state of shock.

Mrs. Muellim felt faint. She sank down onto the stone steps of her house. Fear gripped her heart as she remembered that her earthly treasures were all down at Olsons' house—her blind husband and four of her five children. She looked down the hillside to view the site of the tragedy. She heard excited voices, but in the illumination of the street light she could see that our house was still standing. Come to think of it, her house was less than a block from ours. Why hadn't she heard the explosion? Surely, she thought, she would have heard something if an explosion of the magnitude to which Jamili referred had occurred. Had she misunderstood Jamili? In any case, sitting there contemplating a possible misfortune wasn't helping anyone, so Mrs. Muellim mustered up her courage and rushed down to the Adventists' house to investigate for herself.

THE EXPLOSION ???!!!

In the meantime, pandemonium reigned supreme at our house. Three girls escaped through an outside door behind the pulpit which opened onto nothing but space. Workmen had torn down the balcony and were in the process of building a stairwell. Balancing themselves precariously, the teenage girls negotiated the six-inch wide masonry wall to a ladder where they climbed down the one story to the ground. Ordinarily this was a feat that none of them could have accomplished even in broad daylight. It was amazing that none of them fell.

At the other end of the hallway, people rushed through the open French doors of our living room and out onto the south veranda. There they trembled with fear waiting for the explosion. When nothing happened after a few minutes, one of the newcomers, a young man from Bishmizeen, decided he'd act as city marshal. He whipped out his pistol and started into the dark meeting hall to "kill Mr. Olson's assassin." The Akar and Muellim girls told him that was dangerous. In the darkness no one could distinguish one person from another. When he insisted upon carrying out his plan, the girls grabbed him around the waist and hung on. He dragged them around the veranda behind him, trying to rid himself of the leeches. Fortunately, the girls never gave up, and he never got into the house to use his gun.

A new groom locked himself in our kitchen and refused to let anyone else in for fear it might be the attacker. His bride was one of those who knocked on the door pleading for admittance, but he refused to open the door to anyone lest it be the hit man. In a matter of seconds, the group had stumbled through the maze of upset chairs and out the front door—which wasn't hard now with all of the screen gone.

Moses and I knew that no person had cut off the electricity—the problem was only a burned out fuse. We thought that if we continued to carry on the song service as usual, it would engender a calming affect upon the audience. Well, so much for our reasoning. We had not seen mass mania in action before.

I had sat on the organ stool in the aisle, as usual. (We could get in more people by putting the chairs in rows with an aisle along each wall. The back of the organ was against one wall near the middle of the hall. It took out a few chair spaces there and made the opening very narrow.) I continued to play the organ, and Moses continued to sing, but no one paid any attention to our efforts. As the people dashed by me frantically feeling their way in the darkness for exits, they poked their fingers in my eyes and ears, scratched my face, and snagged my hair. I forgave them the scratches and the hair loss since I knew it wasn't easy to push their way around me; but when they kicked the stool out from under me, THAT did it! No longer would I act like a hero on a sinking ship. I crawled to the end of the organ away from the flow of traffic and scrunched myself into that protected niche.

A second later I heard a thud, and Moses stopped singing. I wondered what had happened to him. It certainly would not surprise me if someone got killed in the stampede, but I didn't want it to be Moses. He had worked with us for two years, and we had grown very fond of him.

In less time than it takes to tell, everyone was either out or dead or injured, and the house became deathly still. Wayne emerged from his office door and shouted, "Everyone stay where you are. A fuse has blown, and I'm going to the bedroom to get a flashlight. I'll have the lights on in just a few minutes."

Across the hallway from me a pitiful voice pleaded, "Will someone please tell me what is happening? Every

THE EXPLOSION ???!!!

time I grab someone and ask them why the screaming and running, they shove me away and yell, 'Don't kill me'. Everyone is acting plumb crazy! I just want to know what's going on." The voice was that of Mr. Muellim, the blind man. "So far I've lost my cane and fez (hat), and they finally knocked me down too."

"Just stay where you are now, Mr. Muellim," I called. "The fan blew a fuse, the lights went out, and people got scared and ran. Wayne is going to put in a new fuse now. Then we'll get things straightened around again."

The scenario struck me as being very humorous, and I laughed to myself. Mr. Muellim, being blind, hadn't seen the smoke nor the lights go out. He was literally "in the dark" no matter how you thought of it.

Wayne came out of the bedroom with the flashlight. Oh, how good that glimmer of light seemed!

Just then someone dashed through the front door yelling, "Don't move! DON'T ANYONE MOVE, or I'll split your head open with my stick!" He walked menacingly toward Wayne who obviously had not listened to his warning and was moving. My frenzied heart made some turbulent twists. "Oh, no! Don't ruin Wayne's head," I whimpered aloud.

Wayne quickly flashed the light in the man's eyes, temporarily blinding him. That was long enough for Wayne to recognize the stick-wielder as our friend. "It's ME, Mr. Akar. Wayne Olson!" Wayne said calmly. "I'm safe, and everyone else will be too, if you'll just put your stick down. Don't hit me!"

"Yeah, don't hit him," I chimed in from my corner, but no one heard me.

"It's you, Wayne?" questioned Mr. Akar. "You're alive?"

"As near as I can tell," Wayne answered.

"Well, so you are! So you are!! Let me go after your enemy."

"There is no enemy," Wayne grabbed Mr. Akar's arm.

"But I heard screaming, lots of it!" Mr. Akar's shop was just half a block down the main street from us.

"Sure you did. People panicked when the fan blew a fuse and the lights went out. But no one killed anyone. Now come with me, Mr. Akar, and we'll replace the fuse."

As Wayne made his way to the utility room, he flashed the light around the hall. He was relieved not to see anyone lying under the chairs. Then we heard Moses groan. Wayne flashed the light in his direction. "Moses, are you hurt?"

"Pa—l—ease, p—pull the boy off," Moses begged, obviously short of breath. And no wonder! There, clinging to Moses with all his strength and pushing his head as far as possible into Moses' abdomen, was the little crippled boy. When the lights went out, the boy was scared spitless because he feared he couldn't hobble out in time to escape the explosion. In the darkness, he detected this person in white and clung to him as if he were his guardian angel. We finally pulled him off of Moses.

"That's the last time I'll wear white," Moses commented as he sucked in air. "Now get this chalk board off my neck. Someone kicked it off its stand, and it whacked me a good one. I couldn't move to get it off with this little octopus squeezing me."

Wayne set the chalkboard on the floor while Moses examined the knot on his head. Then Wayne and Mr. Akar replaced the main fuse, and the house was ablaze with light. The six of us left in the house—Moses, Wayne, the blind man, Mr. Akar, the crippled boy, and

THE EXPLOSION ???!!!

myself—examined the damage. Outside of the broken screen doors and the upset chairs scattered in all directions, there seemed to be no property damage. However, we were worried about the people. How badly were they injured from their flight?

Gradually people crept back into the meeting place. Wayne asked them to set the chairs up in rows and sit down so he could preach his evening's sermon.

When everyone was seated again, and it was determined that no one was injured other than bruises on their legs from kicking the chairs, Wayne gave them a brief lecture. "You folks came here tonight expecting trouble, and you got it—not from an enemy, but from your own apprehensions. When the lights went out, you all panicked and ran. Thank God no one was hurt. Next time, let's put our trust in God."

The audience was exceptionally quiet that evening as Wayne presented the sermon. I felt I needed a breath of fresh air so I went and stood by the screen door, still hanging by a hinge. I thought I had had enough excitement for one night until Rafic, Jamili's husband, came charging across the street in his underwear—or what was left of it. He had been relaxing in his baggy Arab underpants when Jamili staggered into their living room and dropped onto the sofa. Rafic was naturally alarmed at his wife's appearance. He jumped up and put wet cloths on her forehead until she could cool down and speak. She told him the story of the explosion at the Olsons' house, and how only she had escaped.

"I am so thankful that you got out alive, my Darling," Rafic said patting her hand. "Now just try to calm down, and I will get you a cup of tea. I am so sorry for those from our village who lost their lives down.... JUST A MINUTE! Jamili, where are our six children? Weren't most of them down at the meeting with you?"

"Yes. YES, they were!" Jamili bolted into a sitting position, then dropped back on the couch. "Oh, woe is me! Are we left childless?" Jamili moaned.

Rafic needed to hear no more. He sprung from his chair and vaulted down the hillside, ripping his loose, flowing underwear as he leaped over stone wall terraces. When he reached our door he was quaking from fear and exhaustion. He was also a sight to behold. His hair stood on end, he dripped with perspiration, and his face was contorted. His underwear was in shreds, exposing parts of his body not ordinarily on display.

I stopped him at the top of the steps. "You can't come in looking like that," I said, keeping my vision above his head. "You'll embarrass all of us."

"B—but, my children. I need to save my children-pull them out from the rubble." Rafic wept.

"There is no rubble, Rafic," I said calmly.

"B—but, the explosion! Jamili said…"

"There was no explosion. See for yourself. Everyone is sitting peacefully listening to the sermon." I still kept my vision high. The condition of his underwear was pitiful.

Rafic stared in disbelief. "I, ah, see. Your house is still intact. No damage anywhere. Everyone sitting quietly in chairs." Then he walked slowly down the steps shaking his head. "Woe is me! My Jamili has gone stark raving mad. I knew God would punish me for not going to church."

Mr. Akar met Rafic at the foot of the steps and drew him into the shadows. "For shame, Rafic, coming down here barefoot and, aaah, in your und—well, basically bare. You're a wealthy, respected citizen of this town. You can't stay here looking like this!"

"But I rushed down here to find my children. Jamili told me that the Adventist house had blown up and only

THE EXPLOSION ???!!!

she escaped. Let me tell you, friend, I don't know what to do about Jamili. She's gone crazy." Rafic cried.

Mr. Akar explained the whole situation to Rafic to put his mind at rest. He persuaded him there was nothing wrong with Jamili except hysteria. She had just over-reacted. Then a very much humiliated Rafic took off through the dark alleys for his home.

The next day everyone in the village was laughing about the explosion that wasn't. A number of them were limping about nursing their bruises. But Jamili's bruises topped them all—her legs were by far the most colorful.

Never again did we face opposition in Farhazier. I hoped this tranquility would spread throughout the entire area of our labor. But Satan was not willing to give up his territory without another fight.

Hallway of our home in Fahazier. Weekly meetings of about 60 people gathered here.

Midge, Moses, Farris, Wayne, Noel, Ruby and Michael are on the platform ready to begin meetings in Bishmizeen.

CHAPTER 22

THE BATTLE FOR BISHMIZEEN

We hadn't expected trouble in Bishmizeen, but it came anyway.

Early in June of 1950, we rented the ideal spot in which to hold our evangelistic effort. Our friend, Rita, owned a vacant lot 110 x 150 feet behind her house. It was enclosed on all sides by stone walls or houses of friends. The only entrance from the street was the walkway between two houses. A gate at the far end of the property led to the back yard of Abu Hanni, one of our Bible students. A side and back door from Rita's house were the only other places of access into this area. We were taking reasonable precautions just in case persecution should raise its ugly head again.

Our whole staff was excited about the Bishmizeen meetings. I was especially pleased that the mission had hired two lady Bible workers to help us—Ruby Williams, a teacher from Canada on loan to us from MEC for the summer, and Noel Abdul Messiah, a young Bible worker intern from Iraq. They rented two large rooms from Rita; one room had the back door which opened conveniently into our meeting area. Michael Kebbas also moved to Bishmizeen. These workers started visiting in the homes of the villagers before our meetings started to establish new friendships. We already had a number of acquaintances in Bishmizeen from the meetings we had in Nabti's home. They were the ones who requested that we hold an effort.

MIDGE IN LEBANON

Moses, who commuted from Shekka to help with the effort, repainted the back drops for the platform. I improved the looks of the podium by fastening lush red satin around its periphery and setting that off with a gold fringe. It looked like a piece of furniture right out of the Moses' wilderness Tabernacle.

We began our meetings Sunday night, July 9, with over 200 in attendance. The same interest continued through the Wednesday and Friday nights meetings.

The second Sunday night we sensed that trouble was in the offing when four teenage boys sauntered into our arena a bit early. They seated themselves on the left front row near the organ and formed a huddle. They seemed to be conspiring together on some issue. We soon discovered that heckling us was their goal. Two of them were altar boys in the village church, and the priest had sent them to disturb our meeting in any way they could. They chose a very unique way to do this.

The four boys had beautiful singing voices. However, they amused themselves and disturbed us by singing secular songs while Moses led the audience in singing hymns. Protestant hymns, written in a major key, were a new experience for the people of the village who were accustomed to chanting church responses in a minor key. Therefore, the audience hesitated to sing loudly while the boys belted out their songs in the ten decibel range. This distressed Moses; he could not be heard above them. The boys frustrated me as well. They were sitting directly behind me, and I couldn't hear if I was playing the right notes on the organ; I couldn't hear Moses, either.

When the preaching began, the boys laughed and talked occasionally, but, in general, they appeared to be listening. I sat down on the end of the front row and looked at them from the corner of my eye, trying to size

THE BATTLE FOR BISHMIZEEN

them up. They were nice looking boys in their late teens, obviously intelligent and talented. I had no idea that the priest had sent them, but I knew they could be excellent candidates for God's kingdom. I resolved to make these boys our friends.

After the meeting I introduced myself. "I'm Mrs. Olson," I said. "I notice that you young men have excellent voices. We surely could use you to sing special music for the meetings."

The boys looked at each other and grinned sheepishly. They were pleased with my compliment and mumbled some recognition of the fact. Then I suggested that they stay and learn a special song to sing at our next meeting. Moses looked askance. I could tell he was not thrilled with my idea.

I handed the young men an Arabic hymnal, and they perused it until they finally selected a song that they thought had nice poetry and meaning. I played the hymn on the organ, and Moses helped them learn the melody. Soon two of them were harmonizing, and it sounded wonderful. Their voices were so melodious that their music gave me goose, bumps. They were pleased with themselves and promised to come early for practice before the next meeting. That night we gained four friends; though the priest didn't know it yet, he had lost two altar boys.

Of course, the priest soon learned that his boys were singing for us. Only the imagination can fathom the anger that raged within the old man's breast. He determined he would send us packing from Bishmizeen by dumping a good dose of his wrath upon us. He had tolerated us for a month; now he would force us to stop.

Wednesday afternoon, August 9, the priest and Henry Jeha, a young political leader, organized a mob to attack us that night. They instructed their men to arm themselves anyway they liked but particularly to bring buckets filled with baseball-size stones and tin cans. They agreed that when the priest rang the bell, they would assemble at the church, walk the one block to our meeting place, and attack en masse. They were to hurl their stones over the roofs of the houses into our enclosure. The priest charged them, "Let the stones fall where they may. Anyone injured receives his just dessert."

No one leaked the plan to us, but experience taught us to be on the alert. When Wayne heard the church bell ring, he instinctively knew it signaled trouble. He hurriedly finished his sermon, had prayer, and dismissed the people just as the mob was coming down the street beating on tin cans and chanting death threats. At the close of each meeting, Wayne usually showed a filmstrip that reviewed the subject he had just presented, but he omitted it this night. Stealthily the people slipped out through the walkway, Abu Hanni's garden gate, or the doors of Rita's house. When the mob arrived, they were quite disappointed that there was no one left to stone. We knew they would lay better plans for the next night.

What we didn't know was that they were laying for us on the road that night. After we turned out the lights in the meeting area, we stayed and chatted with Noel and Ruby. Farris hopped on Moses' motorcycle with him, and the two headed for Farhazier. In a few minutes we heard several shots fired in the direction the boys had gone. Our hearts beat wildly with fear. Wayne and I jumped in our car and drove down the road to investigate. (In retrospect, that was a foolish thing to do.) About half a mile down the road we saw a figure in white lying by the roadside. "It's Moses," I gasped. "He wears white."

THE BATTLE FOR BISHMIZEEN

We came to a screeching halt. When we stopped, the person arose and fired several shots over our car. It was not Moses. Wayne backed the car up and shined his headlights on the highway men. (Again a foolish thing to do.) This temporarily blinded them, and we got a good look at them—good enough to be able to identify them by name. The five slipped back down into the ditch, and we drove on. They hadn't planned to kill anyone, I don't believe, just intimidate us. Yet it was hardly an experience to enjoy just before bedtime.

Friday night Wayne began the meeting with the filmstrip he had omitted on Wednesday night. In a few minutes, we heard the mob coming down the street, beating on tin cans, and chanting eerily. It sent shivers down my back. Then stones hurtled into our meeting place. Some of them were aimed at the platform where Wayne and Farris should have been standing. As the stones rained in on us, some bounced off the empty platform and plywood screen, some dented the organ or pulpit, while others landed in the aisles. Not a person was hit! This was miraculous, considering the piles of stones they had thrown.

Wayne stood by the projector and called for everyone to remain calm. "You must forgive our persecutors," he said. "Most of those in the mob don't know what we teach; so please, hold no grudge nor a desire for revenge against your fellow villagers."

After Wayne's speech, the stones poured down around us, and the people began to panic. Immediately Ruby and Noel invited them to take shelter in their two rooms which adjoined the meeting area. We all raced into their house and closed the shutters so the stones could not come through the open windows.

Just before the attack, Henry Jeha, one of the mob organizers, came into our enclosure and leaned against

MIDGE IN LEBANON

the wall out of the reach of the stones. He wanted to observe the success of their assault upon us. He was awed as he watched the stones, seemingly guided by an unseen hand, land in the aisles, missing everyone. He got the strange sensation that God was protecting the Adventists and their friends in a miraculous way, and that he, like Saul, was working against God. When he saw Wayne's forgiving spirit and courage under duress, he felt impressed that he must learn more about Adventists. Secretly, of course!

After we were safely secured in the rooms of the Bible workers' house, Wayne put Farris and Moses in charge, jumped in his car, and drove to Amuin. He was not surprised when he walked into the county sheriffs office and found only a flunky at the switchboard. Obviously "someone" had arranged to have all of the police force out of the office that night. All Wayne could do was to file a complaint and request police protection for our next meeting on Sunday night.

Sabbath was a happy day in spite of the concerns we had for our Sunday night meeting in Bishmizeen. We had special prayer and left it in the hands of God. We had come to depend completely upon His protection and guidance. God constantly surprised us by the way He chose to deliver us from our enemies.

Sabbath afternoon was always a busy time. Some of our workers and church members went to Ras Muska for the branch Sabbath School at Deeb's house; others went way up the mountain for a church service at the Obeids' home; still others stayed in the area and made visits. Rose, a girl who was living with us to learn English, and I stayed in Farhazier that Sabbath to clean up from the big dinner we had served our many guests. At four we conducted the MV meeting.

THE BATTLE FOR BISHMIZEEN

Rose and I were bushed when night came. We put the children to bed and sat down in the living room to relax. We knew Wayne wouldn't be home until late since he had gone to a village north of Tripoli. We had no Saturday night games planned for that week, either, so we were rather surprised when someone knocked on our door about eight o'clock. I was so tired I really didn't want to be bothered with guests, but I went to the door anyway. I became apprehensive when I saw who it was. There stood the police captain accompanied by a doctor from Amuin. I suspected they were up to no good; they both had guilty looks on their faces. Immediately God impressed me not to talk to them in Arabic, even though the temptation was very great. So, I simply motioned the men into the house.

The men entered and introduced themselves. Then the captain said to me in Arabic, "Your husband is not here, is he?" I could have questioned how he knew that, but with informants all over the place, this was not astonishing.

"Rose," I called in English, "come here, please. There are two men at the door, and I need you to translate for me."

Rose came out of the living room looking perplexed. "Why, Mrs. Olson? You know Arabic well. Why should I trans..."

"Rose, don't ask questions now! God will show me why I'm doing this later, and then we'll discuss it. For now, TRANSLATE!"

When the men noted that I called for Rose, they concluded that I did not know Arabic. They conversed privately with her, asking again if Mr. Olson was home. Rose assured them he was not. Then the captain replied, "Good! We came here specifically at this time because we heard he would definitely not be here. So we're in luck. Now tell Mrs. Olson to inform her husband that he must NOT hold any more meetings in Bishmizeen! I will not provide them with police protection."

Rose translated the message to me.

"Tell them to come into the living room and explain this to me more fully," I said, hedging for time. I sensed there was something irregular about their visit; therefore, I formulated a plan to trap them. The two men had come calling on two women who were neither close friends nor relatives of theirs, and at a time when they knew the man of the house was not home. This is taboo in Arab culture. When the two men walked into our living room, they entrapped themselves even more. I had them just where I wanted them.

Poor Rose dragged along behind me looking completely bewildered. "They shouldn't come in, Mrs. Olson. This is not appropriate," she whispered.

"Go along with me, Rose," I said out of the side of my mouth. "Invite them to relax in the easy chairs while I get a cool drink and cookies." (This had become my standard method of diverting the policemen's attention from their errand.) "Tell them I will send for Farris. They can explain it to him."

Rose translated my message.

"Oh, no! No, don't call Farris. Just deliver our message to Mr. Olson," the captain insisted adamantly. Rose translated, and we sat quietly for a spell.

Then the doctor began flirting with Rose. "My, you are a pretty girl. I suppose the men are always after you. How many boyfriends do you have?"

Rose was flustered by his overt attention and didn't know how to answer him. She glanced at me for help, but I just smiled and looked as ignorant as possible.

THE BATTLE FOR BISHMIZEEN

Inside, I was seething because of the lustful way he looked at Rose.

Then the captain joined in the game. "Mrs. Olson is also an attractive lady. Imagine our good fortune to be invited to spend part of the night with these lovely ladies." They said much more which I won't repeat.

I was furious by their remarks, but I think I managed to conceal it. "Excuse me, I'll go to the kitchen for some lemonade," I suggested pleasantly. Rose translated my message, but her eyes said, "Don't leave me!"

"That would be nice," the doctor agreed. Rose repeated it, and I left for the kitchen. On the way I called to our landlord from our bedroom balcony, "Send Tony to get Farris right away, please. Tell him the police captain is here."

Everyone knew where Farris would be on Saturday nights—up at the Akars visiting his love, Laurice. Evidently Tony made immediate contact, because just as I finished serving our guests the lemonade and cookies, Farris burst through the door. "What is the problem here, Mrs. Olson?" Farris called as he rushed into the living room.

Both men jumped at the sight of Farris. "Oh, aah, nothing, they stuttered. "We, ah, we just stopped by to tell her that you folks must cancel the meetings in Bishmizeen. We cannot protect you. Orders from headquarter, you know."

Then I launched into a tirade in Arabic. "Orders from headquarters, NOTHING! We have our permit from the government which entities us to preach in all of Lebanon. This includes police protection. You thought to trick us by delivering your message to me, a woman. You thought that would take you off the hook if my husband persisted in preaching and there was trouble.

MIDGE IN LEBANON

You thought you could excuse yourself to the authorities because you had warned ME, and my husband didn't listen. Right?"

Rose was confused again because, when Farris arrived, I instantly found my Arabic tongue. Now Rose had lost hers; all she could do was nod.

The two men turned pale. "You understood us when we talked to the girl?" they queried, obviously shaken. Suddenly their arrogance was gone, and they were willing to play ball in my court.

"Yes, I understood everything you said." I turned to Farris. "What is the penalty for an officer of the law who enters the home of a woman when the husband is not present? He insulted us by dishonoring a good Arabic custom."

"Oh, please, Mrs. Olson, we did not mean to..." the captain pleaded.

"Yes, you did," I insisted accusingly. "You specifically said you came here at a time when you knew my husband was not home. Didn't he, Rose?"

Rose nodded.

"What is more," I continued, "his doctor friend sat here and made lewd remarks to Rose and me."

Rose nodded again.

"Now, I ask you, Farris, what will the government do with this captain if I should report him? He didn't even want me to send for you."

By this time, Farris was galled by the actions of these two, supposedly responsible, men. Farris had barely launched his lecture when the captain interrupted. "What can we do to reach an understanding?"

"Give us police protection for our meetings," I demanded. "I am not asking for favors. That is the right of free people everywhere. My husband will be over at your office in the morning, and you can tell him about your arrangements. I'll accept nothing less. Goodnight, gentlemen."

The captain and the doctor left, defeated men. By flaunting an honorable Arabic custom, they had been caught in their own web. We suspected the captain had been bribed by those opposing our meetings. It was his duty to protect people from religious persecution, and he knew it. I hadn't planned this confrontation, but Farris, Rose, and I believed God had His hand in it.

The next morning the captain was waiting in his office to see Wayne. "Your wife is very strong," he observed wryly.

Wayne wanted to laugh, but he didn't. "How many men will you have in Bishmizeen tonight?" he asked simply.

"Enough, if I find transportation." The captain wasn't too conciliatory.

"I'll be by to pick up your force about seven," Wayne promised and left.

Sunday evening, August 13, Wayne brought the captain and one gendarme (state policeman) to Bishmizeen. When they stepped out of the car, they met 20 or more men milling about the Village Square which was right outside the entry to our meeting place. The captain ordered the crowd to disperse, but they were defiant.

The first one to confront the captain was the big, strapping Communist leader (Wayne's "protector" in Farhazier who bolted through our screen door). He challenged the captain, "Don't you get pushy with me. This is my village, and I'll walk in the streets anytime I want to. So there!"

The two officers hardly dared refute that statement; they were greatly outnumbered by the villagers. The captain was angered, but he contained his wrath congenially for self-preservation. The crowd left us alone that night and got their entertainment by heckling the police.

Was it chance or providence that brought the district's representative in parliament, Mr. Badir, back to his home town that night? Mr. Badir heard the disturbance from his costly home which was only a block from the Village Square.

"I'm hearing some commotion down in the village. Does anyone know what it is all about?" Mr. Badir asked.

"Oh, the Adventists have come to town, and the priest along with some others oppose them. Olson preaches salvation by faith," a supporter volunteered.

"Well now, that is a simple matter. I can solve it instantly." He called his servant. "Ahid, go tell the people in the street to go quietly home now. Assure them there will be no more Adventist meetings in this town. I'll call Mr. Olson to my home tomorrow and tell him to withdraw from Bishmizeen."

The order was promptly delivered by his servant. The people dispersed and went home, much to the relief of the captain. After the meeting, Wayne was informed that he should appear before Mr. Badir in the morning.

Oh, the prayers we prayed in North Lebanon! Sometimes we wondered if God would get weary of hearing from us. It seemed that our line to heaven was always overloaded with supplications, but where else could we turn?

Wayne went to the home of Mr. Badir the next day with trepidation. We humans are such tenuous creatures. Even though we pray and trust in God, there

THE BATTLE FOR BISHMIZEEN

remains a degree of fear when it comes right down to the wire. This is especially true when one must appear before an influential potentate like Mr. Badir. Wayne knew the future of the Adventist mission in North Lebanon depended on the outcome of this interview. The terrible responsibility of this was almost overwhelming. He was thankful he could depend upon God's still small voice, speaking to his mind, to give him the right words to say.

Wayne was ushered into Mr. Badir's formal reception room. He was astonished that Mr. Badir had bolstered his position by having present the mayor, the city councilmen, and other important people. It must have appeared to those men that Wayne stood alone, but Wayne was supported by **THE COUNSELOR** who has power over the district representative and all other earthly rulers.

At first the conversation between Mr. Badir and Wayne was casual and friendly. Then the representative got to the point. "I have heard that your preaching here is dividing the village. The majority of the people do not want you here, so I am ordering you to stop your meetings immediately."

We had heard this would be his demand, so Wayne was prepared. We had prayed the matter through already and knew this was not acceptable. If we withdrew from Bishmizeen it would set a precedent that could shut down all the work in North Lebanon for years to come. The opposition would be strengthened by their success and extend their power, Furthermore, what would happen to those who were already baptized Adventists? They were still babes in the faith and needed more nurturing. No, we couldn't leave Bishmizeen.

Wayne chose his words carefully. "Mr. Badir, I respect your request, but I believe you have not been presented with all of the facts. We meet quietly in a private yard and do not bother anyone. Anyone is welcome to come to our meetings, but we do not force them..."

"No, but you entice them by showing pictures and giving away books and Bibles," Mr. Badir argued. He looked around for support and heads nodded.

"But surely you, as a Christian, approve of our giving away Bibles. Jesus told us to preach the gospel in all the world, and that is what I'm doing."

"Oh, don't talk to us about preaching the gospel. Our Christian church can trace its roots back to the Apostles and Jesus. We were Christians here when you in America were still a bunch of naked Indians running around." This brought a chuckle from his retinue, and Mr. Badir grinned with satisfaction at his "joke."

"But we teach the gospel directly from the Bible," Wayne contended. "We are not teaching any traditions that a particular church might have developed over the past 1900 years."

Mr. Badir realized that he was dealing with one who knew the Bible far better than did he or any of his supporters, so he changed his tactics. "All right. So a few have chosen to go to your meetings, but the majority want you out."

"What about those who want to hear more from the Bible? Shouldn't they have the freedom to hear?" Wayne asked politely.

"NO! You should respect the rights of the majority. They don't want your meetings here!" Mr. Badir reiterated, becoming more adamant.

"Is that what Jesus did?" Wayne countered. "When He was here on earth, did the majority want Him or accept Him? They cried, 'Crucify Him!' Suppose Christ would

THE BATTLE FOR BISHMIZEEN

have used your line of reasoning and concluded, 'Since the majority of the people do not want me here, I will respect their desires and return to heaven without dying for their sins.' If He had done that, what hope of salvation would we have today?"

Mr. Badir ignored Wayne's logic. Pride, politics, and prejudice prevented him from changing his position. "Leave Christ out of this! Do what the majority wants!" he demanded irately. "If you do not stop your meetings, I'll have the Adventists thrown out of all of Lebanon!"

This threat—throwing Adventists out of ALL of Lebanon—presented a broader dimension of consequences than Wayne expected. Would his refusal to obey Mr. Badir's order jeopardize ALL the mission's work in Lebanon-Middle East College, the Bible Correspondence School, Middle East Press, the Middle East Union, the local mission, and the schools in the Beirut area? Furthermore, would it spell doom for the work in the Middle East in general? Lebanon was about to become the headquarters for the proposed Middle East Division.

Wayne considered the seriousness of the decision he must now make. Would it be better to "shake the dust from his feet" and retire to safer territory, thus insuring the security of the work in the rest of Lebanon? As Wayne prayed silently, he remembered that God had fulfilled His promise by giving us souls for His kingdom in North Lebanon and had protected us miraculously while we worked. Surely God did not want Wayne to submit to Mr. Badir's request and quit now.

Wayne knew his refusal would challenge and humiliate Mr. Badir in front of his constituents. Wayne would rather have spoken to him privately so the representative could save face. But Mr. Badir had set himself up by bringing in the auspicious clientele to witness his authority. Everyone waited confidently for Wayne's submissive response; but God had the final word.

"I'm sorry, Sir. I cannot leave Christ aside. I must follow His example and continue to preach the gospel to those who want to hear it in Bishmizeen."

The men sucked in their breath—David had challenged Goliath. Mr. Badir was stunned that Wayne dared refuse to subject himself and God's work to his authority. He was still in shock as Wayne shook his limp hand and calmly left the room.

During the next few days, we waited anxiously to know if Mr. Badir was able to persuade the Lebanese Parliament members to vote against us. Our people prayed that God would curtail the power of this modern pharaoh. God did; we received no directives from the parliament in Beirut.

On Wednesday night we proceeded with our meetings as usual. Wayne went to Amuin and picked up the captain and four gendarmes. The captain stationed two gendarmes at the entrance to the walkway and two more at Abu Hanni's gate. The four men faithfully executed their duties, and, at the same time, enjoyed a very enlightening lecture on the Sabbath. The crowd out front continued to heckle the captain; his evening hadn't been pleasant at all. On Friday night the captain endured even more taunts.

As I came through the walkway on Friday night, I noticed one of the town's "toughs" leaning against the stone wall. I walked over to him and extended my hand to greet him (better to curry his friendship right away, I thought), but he did not respond. That signaled a redflag warning to me. Worse yet, when I got to the other side of him, I noticed he was clutching a knife, which was almost concealed, under his folded arm. That kept me uneasy most of the night. I was relieved when the

THE BATTLE FOR BISHMIZEEN

meeting was over and the "Tough Boy" left without using his weapon. Later I learned he was there to take revenge upon a man. It seems that one of our trouble makers was his enemy. Just in case our mutual foe caused us any trouble, he could fight him, using the excuse that he was trying to protect the Adventists. I could have enjoyed the evening more if I'd only known that to begin with. In any case, we had no trouble that night, but the mob on the street had vexed the captain into a froth.

"Don't bother to come for us on Sunday night," the captain said through clenched teeth. "I'll bring my men over in a government jeep."

We hoped he wouldn't forget, and he didn't. Early Sunday night he drove up in his jeep with seven gendarmes. He promptly went to a nearby store and asked the owner to keep the public telephone free. He added, "I have orders to call out the forces from Tripoli in case there is any trouble here tonight."

(Imagine an Adventist evangelist preaching the gospel while he is guarded by a whole unit of state police. Amazingly, it had come to this.)

The store owner made sure that the captain's threat was leaked to the ruffians on the street. The few die-hards that still persisted in disrupting the peace disappeared into the night. There was absolutely no disturbance in Bishmizeen that night nor any of the nights that followed. The government had stepped in to preserve religious freedom, and they meant business. The people got the message, and so did Mr. Badir—there was Someone more powerful than he.

The battle for Bishmizeen was over, and God's cause had triumphed.

MIDGE IN LEBANON

* * * * * *

Satan's intent in bringing sickness, sorrow, death, disappointment, suffering and persecution upon God's children is to cause God pain. It's his way of taking revenge upon the One who cast him out of heaven. Since the beginning, Satan has used religious and political leaders to suppress the free study of God's Word and to persecute those who teach it. He used the same tactics to rout our work in North Lebanon. He didn't succeed.

For centuries the people of this area had followed the traditions and dogmas established by their churches. But many were dissatisfied with the rituals and masses; they longed to hear of a compassionate God who understood their humanity. They were happy to learn of God's simple plan for their salvation. This is why we had to risk our lives, stay in North Lebanon, and teach the Bible—to satisfy the yearning of those who had the courage to break with traditions and family.

Politics in Lebanon usually prospers in the gloved hand of religion. Political candidates who are sanctioned by the church will win the elections since all of their members are urged to vote accordingly. Thus, a politician is obligated to the clergy for his position and will remain in power as long as he fulfills the dictates of his benefactors.

Mr. Badir was possibly caught in this net. However, he defied the living God by demanding, "Put Christ aside. Leave Him out of this. Do what the majority wants." These words were recorded in heaven. God is not vindictive, but there are times when He must interfere to preserve truth. When His control is needed, He sets up rulers and removes them.

Mr. Badir died a few month's after his confrontation with Wayne. We were sorry for his demise and attended

THE BATTLE FOR BISHMIZEEN

his funeral. I wished we could have known that he repented of his careless attitude toward God.

In 1954 an Adventist church and school was built less than a block from the home of the late Mr. Badir. This church remains as a witness to the God who humbles rulers when they overstep their authority by defying their Creator and Sustainer. And yes, the pulpit, nicked by the stones thrown in Bishmizeen, stands in a back room of the church as a mute reminder of the battle that was won.

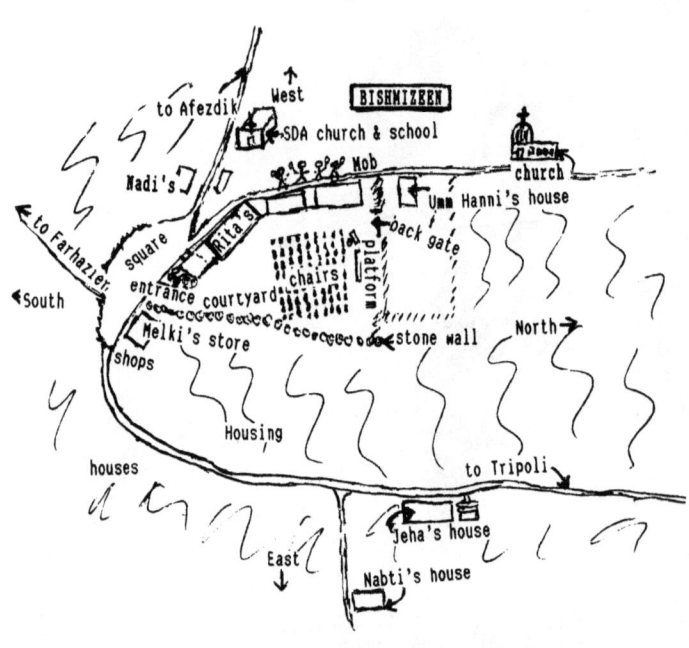

CHAPTER 23

AFTER THE BATTLE

The meetings in Bishmizeen were over in mid-September. It had been a battle of sorts, but the trophies gained for God's kingdom made it well worth the struggle. Um and Abu Hanni were among the first to accept the message. This sweet old couple had been looking for explanations to their questions for years. They were thrilled to learn what the Bible taught about the state of the dead, the Sabbath, and many other points of Bible doctrine. Previous to the Bible studies, their minds had been in turmoil over questions for which no one seemed to have answers.

"Now, I have complete peace because I understand the Bible and God who inspired men to record it," Um Hanni said confidently as she patted the Bible she held on her lap. "Salvation is a gift of God—nothing I have to earn. Heaven is a real place inhabited by real people—not just a place for nebulous spirits bored stiff from floating around. Jesus went to heaven in a real body, an immortal one, and so will I. I love the thought of having feet to walk the streets of gold, hands to pluck the never-fading flowers, lips to smile at Jesus, and fingers to touch Him."

I shall never forget the day Wayne baptized Um Hanni in Jonah's Bay. She came up out of the water praising the Lord. She knelt on the sand and bowed her head in prayer. "Thank you, Jesus. You have just washed away all my sins in the sea, and there they can stay. Thank you for the knowledge of your saving love. I'm ready to meet you anytime now. Amen."

When we held the first communion service after the baptism, Um Hanni insisted upon washing my feet. Why? She quoted from Isaiah 52:7. "'How beautiful upon the mountain are the feet of him that bringeth good tidings, that publisheth peace;...that publisheth salvation; that saith to Zion, thy God reigneth.' Sister Olson, your feet brought the good news of salvation to our mountain; therefore, they are beautiful feet. You and Brother Olson risked your lives to teach the pure Biblical truth that I had longed to hear. Now that knowledge is mine, and it has brought tranquility to my soul. That's why God sends missionaries!"

We held each other in a long embrace as our tears of love mingled. Um Hanni's words of appreciation eclipsed the days of persecution. This moment of joy was worth it all.

Members of the Jeha family were more gems. Henry, one of the mob organizers, came to us privately asking for Bible studies. "I saw how marvelously God protected you when we stoned you the first night. God guided those stones in such a way they fell only where no one would get hit. It was so miraculous it scared me. I also remember Mr. Olson telling the people not to hold hard feelings toward those who were attacking the congregation but to forgive us. That impressed me. I knew then that God sanctioned your work, and that I was on the wrong side. I'm switching—I want to be on God's side."

Henry's parents and siblings had opposed his political affiliations with the local communists and his involvement in persecuting us. They were, therefore, very happy when Henry invited us to their house. They all joined in the studies and followed the lessons with much interest and enthusiasm. Unfortunately, we were just getting into decision-making doctrines when the time came for Henry to leave for Syria where he planned to teach school. But God had other plans—He loved this ambitious youth, filled with potential. Just before he left for Syria, Henry accidentally broke his arm while working in his father's olive oil press. This forced Henry to stay in Bishmizeen until his arm could heal. This proved to be a blessing—now he had time to complete his Bible studies with us. Henry became so enthusiastic about what he was learning that he wanted to share it with others. He went with Wayne to many of his Bible studies and cottage meetings. That winter Henry helped bring the message to Dar Bishtar and Bziza.

During the next two years, five of the Jehas were baptized—Henry, Esperansa, Elias, Mary, and Afeef. All of them went to Middle East College and became Seventh-day Adventist mission workers. (Some are still in Lebanon teaching in our schools.)

We held meetings in the Nabti home three months before we began the effort in Bishmizeen. Initially, the Nabtis were our strongest supporters in the town. Mike, Selwa, and Najwa attended our meetings regularly. The girls started coming to church in our home in Farhazier on Sabbaths. Mike had a job in Tripoli that involved Sabbath morning work, so he seldom attended church. Mike needed the job because he was saving his money to go to college. In another year he would have the funds on hand for his education. Then, he assured us, he would keep the Sabbath. We tried to encourage him to step out in faith, but he was afraid his boss would fire him.

On Sabbath, September 23, Mike was on his way to work in Tripoli. He was feeling guilty about dishonoring God's Sabbath. As he rode to work, he thought about us worshipping in Farhazier and wished he were with us. He knew his working on Sabbath indicated his lack of faith in the God he really wanted to serve. Halfway to Tripoli, his service taxi had a blowout. (A service taxi functions much the same as a city bus. Service taxis usually have a certain route and charge you only for your seat from point A to point B. These taxis can be hailed anywhere along their route.) Now Mike would be late for work. That did it. Was God trying to tell him something, Mike wondered. He got out of the taxi, crossed the road, and hailed another taxi going back up the mountain to Farhazier.

In the meantime, our Sabbath School members were praying that Mike would have the courage to take his stand for Jesus no matter what the consequences might be. We had scarcely finished praying when Mike walked in the door of our house which also served as our church. We were like Rhoda in the Bible story who could hardly believe her eyes when she answered Peter's knock and recognized him standing at the door. The saints who were praying for Peter's release were so overwhelmed they almost forgot to let him in. At first we were slow to welcome Mike. We could hardly believe our prayers had been answered so quickly. We took a brief recess from Sabbath School and gathered around the object of our prayers. He told us he had made his decision, and we hugged him into the church family.

More amazing still, the Sabbath mail brought a letter from a doctor in California containing a check to help "someone" go to Middle East College. This was the second letter we had received with money for education. We knew who that "someone" could be. The omniscient God impressed a doctor halfway around the world to mail the necessary tuition money three weeks before Mike made his decision. God never ceased to amaze us. We enrolled Mike at MEC the next week. Mike and Najwa Nabti both graduated from MEC and then joined the staff. (After some years they immigrated to America.

AFTER THE BATTLE

Mike is currently working for Stanford University, and Najwa is a librarian in the science/engineering department of the University of Southern California.)

Then there was our sweet singer, George Shahin, the ex-altar boy. He went to MEC and joined the Adventist teaching force for awhile. His younger brother, Samir, also became an Adventist, and has worked for many years in various capacities in the church. At the time of this writing he is the president for the East Mediterranean field.

There were still others in the El-Koura district that joined the church later. Happily, many of the second generation are faithful members. Some are employed church workers while others are active lay people in the church.

Some of those mentioned have died, some are still active in the church, and, sad to say, some have apostatized. Wherever they are, I pray that the lost will return, the dead will be resurrected, and those scattered over the face of the earth will be caught up together with them to meet the Lord in the air. I want to enjoy eternity with our trophies from Bishmizeen when the battle with sin is over.

At the cedars of Lebanon: Nebi, Midge, Wayne, Melod, David and Ronnalee.

CHAPTER 24

POTPOURRI

Pioneering the Adventist work and living in North Lebanon was an incredible and marvelous experience. Each day became a mosaic of events to be imprinted upon our minds forever. We didn't plan for things to happen, they just did. The potpourri that filled our weeks spiced up our lives—sometimes more than we liked.

For instance, we could count on patients coming to us for first aid treatments, but we never knew what medical problems they might bring. One morning during Sabbath School we heard an explosion and a scream. We suspected we would soon see the victim, and we did. In a few minutes a teenage boy knocked urgently at our door. His hand was dripping with blood. He had overloaded the muzzle of his homemade gun with too much powder. When he fired at a small bird in a far-away tree the gun exploded and burned the skin off the back of his hand. We got out the cure-all burn ointment, applied a liberal amount of the salve, and bandaged his hand. He left, and we continued Sabbath School.

There were the rewarding times like the baptisms. Our largest ever was the eight candidates we baptized in June, 1950. In December we had a smaller group. We were now averaging at least two baptismal services per year.

Then there were the social occasions. We often dined with our many friends in the villages—church members and non-members. We reciprocated and enjoyed their company at our dinner table too.

We had happy, care-free times, such as the Saturday night socials. During the rainy, winter months we played party games in our home. During the balmy, rainless summers, we played games on the flat roof of our house or on the public threshing floor. Many non-Adventist youth asked to join with us on these occasions, and we were happy to include them. They thought Adventists had more fun than anyone else, and they wanted a part of it. These socials proved to be a successful evangelistic outreach as well. Many of these fun-loving youth later became Adventists.

We considered active games healthy and harmless, so we amused ourselves with them whenever we played out on the beeader (threshing floor). One moonlit Saturday night Wayne learned that these games were neither healthy nor harmless. The group was playing "Drop-the-Handkerchief". Wayne and a stocky young man were the runners. As they raced around the circle in opposite directions, the elbow of the youth caught Wayne full force in the side and sent him sprawling. Ironically, Wayne had survived all the attempts made on his life—guns, dynamite, and stones—but in a collision with a friend, he ended up with four broken ribs! Obviously, it was safer for Wayne to be out on the firing line.

Sometimes, our evangelistic team planned outings on Mondays. We might picnic up at the cedars of Lebanon, along a river, or by a spring. We might explore a Crusader fortress or the remains of an earlier civilization. During the summer, we often went swimming down at Jonah's Bay where we held our baptisms. The water there was pleasantly warm and was a safe place to swim—except we had to keep an eye on David. He

POTPOURRI

insisted upon jumping into the only place deep enough for us to dive into. No matter how often we rescued him from the water, sputtering and gasping for air, he would always try it again. Since he couldn't, or wouldn't, learn, we tied him to our servant girl who only went in the shallow water where Ronnie played.

We were personally invited to every wedding and engagement party in the village. We had fun associating with the people for these festive events. One Saturday night the Muellim girls came by the house and took Ronnie and David to a wedding celebration. We followed about an hour later. When we arrived in the courtyard, the crowd had formed a circle several people deep around the chairs where the older women were seated. Everyone was singing and clapping merrily to the music of a violinist while someone danced in the center. When I could see over the heads of the people, I was astonished to see that the dancer receiving the accolades was my four-year-old, Ronnalee. Sometime, somewhere, she had learned the folk dance that she was now performing to perfection.

The villagers were very pleased that a member of our family was participating in their festivities. It proved to them that we Americans had amalgamated with their culture and had become one with them. Jesus began his ministry at the wedding feast in Cana; we were continuing our ministry at a wedding feast in Farhazier. Following His example, we honored them by our presence and shared in their joy.

Ronnie completed her dance and then passed the handkerchief to another person. That was the cue for the next one to perform. Some of the Arab folk dances are artistic aerobics with tasteful, graceful movements. The dance Ronnie performed may have been similar to the dance of jubilation done by King David when the Ark of the Covenant entered Jerusalem.

As mentioned earlier, just before the fracas erupted in Bishmizeen, we had received our official government permit to preach. Our original request was to preach in Farhazier IN North Lebanon. When the document arrived, we were astonished. It read "The Seventh-day Adventists have permission to conduct meetings in Farhazier AND North Lebanon. We were ecstatic! This gave us license to teach the Bible everywhere. Providentially, one of the copyists somewhere along the way wrote in the word "AND" instead of "IN". The permit was passed with this small modification. What a world of difference that made to the establishment of our work in North Lebanon. Ever since, we have continued to use that permit.

With the official permit in hand, our team—Farris Bishi, Moses Ghazal, Michael Kebbas, Wayne and I—got overly ambitious. We spread our nets throughout the El-Koura district and beyond: Afesdik, Amuin, Bishmizeen, Bziza, Dar Bishtar, Didee, Farhazier, Halba, Kosba, Ras Muska, Shekka, Tripoli, and a few isolated hamlets. Each place provided us with its own brand of adventures.

Having a permit did not eliminate opposition, as we learned in Bishmizeen. In Ras Muska one family opposed our cottage meetings just to be contrary. They also suspected (correctly) that Moses loved one of the Deeb girls, and they didn't want her to marry anyone outside of the village.

One night when Wayne went out of Deeb's house, he noticed the right rear tire on his car was flat. He thought little of that. Even his sixply tires caved in once in awhile because of the stony country lanes he often traveled. He jacked up the car to change the tire. The car slid right off the jack. Wayne tried again with the same result. Then he examined the rest of the tires and found that three of his four tires had been slashed by a knife. Moses' motor cycle tires had received the same treatment. It took Wayne two hours to patch the inner tubes. By 11:30 that night I had become so worried about him I was about to send out a search party. However, before I could get things organized, Wayne returned home.

Some months later Wayne cashed his monthly pay check in Tripoli. Then he drove out to Deeb's place for the usual 7 p.m. Monday night cottage meeting. The people came, but Deeb, an accountant in Tripoli, did not arrive. Wayne discussed various subjects with the others until 8:30 p.m., then they left.

It was nearing nine when Deeb finally arrived home. Wayne was tired and excused himself to leave, but Deeb insisted that he stay. Deeb apologized for being so late, but pressing business at work had unavoidably detained him. Since there was no telephone in the village, Deeb could not let Wayne know what had happened. After they ate, Wayne and Deeb studied. Wayne didn't leave Deeb's house until 10:30. He finally got home about eleven, dead tired and a bit distraught by the hours he had wasted that night.

The next day Wayne learned why God had made Deeb so late, and why he had been persuaded to stay and study with Deeb even though the hour was very late. Between nine and ten o'clock that night, the very time when Wayne usually traveled the road from Ras Muska to Farhazier, highway robbers had set up a road block. They stole money, watches, and jewelry from the occupants of the cars and buses. Had Wayne been on the road at the usual time, he would have been robbed of his whole month's pay. God knew how desperately we needed our money—every piaster was carefully budgeted for our living expenses or to help some student at MEC. Now we believed Deeb's delay was providential.

There was an interesting sidelight to that highway robbery—one that caught the thieves by surprise. People from the hill and mountain towns go down to Tripoli to get coffins in which to bury their loved ones. Sometimes the body of a person who dies in the city hospital is carried in a coffin back up to the village to be buried with relatives. Therefore, coffins are often carried on the roof racks of buses, either with a body or empty.

On this particular night the last bus in the lineup had a coffin strapped to the rack. Since the bus was overly crowded, some of the young men had climbed up the side ladder on the bus and sat on the roof. It began to drizzle, so one sensible youth crawled into the coffin to keep dry. He braced the lid partly open and fell asleep. He slept through the entire hold-up until one of the gunmen scaled the ladder of his bus. The youth awakened only when he heard the robber yell. He lifted the coffin lid cautiously and peered out at the criminal hanging onto the ladder. The thief was so shocked at seeing the "corpse come to life", that he screamed in fright, fell to the ground, and broke his arm as his gun went off. This bit of bad luck scared the whole robber gang, and they fled in their get-away car. But they had collected enough loot to last them a long time.

Calling on important people was part of the potpourri that spiced up our lives. Sabbath evening, October 28, Wayne and I stopped in Tripoli on our way home from church services at Obeids to visit some important people. Arabs, being the generous and hospitable people that they are, always serve their guests food and drink. In fact, they are sometimes offended if one refuses to eat with them. Spending an entire afternoon making visits

POTPOURRI

could almost guarantee me a net gain of two pounds or a stomach ache. Our host that evening sent out for ice cream. He wanted to honor us with a special treat. Wayne and I were both a bit skeptical about eating the ice cream since we knew it might be made with unpasteurized milk. But with the ice cream melting in the dishes, and the hostess's gracious presentation, we accepted the refreshment and indulged.

About 2 a.m. Wayne and I succumbed to the results of that indulgence. Both of us got deathly ill. Stomach cramps kept us groaning, and diarrhea kept us trotting between the bed and the bathroom. Wayne finally vomited and felt better. I could not. My food had passed beyond where my stomach could recall it. This illness was the catalyst that almost sent me to my death. The amoeba and bacillary dysentery organisms scrambled for commanding positions in my intestines; at the same time, their warfare gave me a good case of colitis. During the next two years I was either in to see a doctor or in the hospital one or more times a month. I was punctured with vitamin and prescription injections. I became the chief source of revenue for the pharmaceutical companies that produced any kind of sulfa drug. I lost so much weight and got so weak that even I, along with my doctors, despaired of my recovery. At first I believed that my inherited stamina and strong constitution was invincible. I thought that my positive attitude and faith in God would keep me alive. I asked God to let me live to raise my children; at the same time, I asked my sister Lela to take them in case of my demise. I was afraid the old devil would use microbes to kill me since he hadn't succeeded in his other attempts. This health problem finally culminated in a heart attack on June 4, 1951. More about this later.

MIDGE IN LEBANON

The deaths and funerals of those I loved left black holes in the mosaic of my life. I knew that death comes to all men, for all have sinned, but I still didn't like it.

A death that almost devastated me was that of six-month-old Kenny Mein. Students at the college built Kenny's little coffin and cleaned the brush from the grave that had been dug for our David during the summer of 1949. On January 30, 1951 we attended Kenny's funeral. At the graveside I relived the agony we had passed through when we waited each day for David to die. I wept uncontrollably; I really sympathized with the Art and Millie over the loss of their child. My weakened physical condition made me less able to cope with emotional stress. Kleins accepted their tragedy valiantly; I didn't handle it as well.

I kept wondering, "Why did David live and Kenny die?" Then the Russells sang the song, "Sometime We'll Understand". The words of that song comforted me: "Not now, but in the coming years, it may be in the better land, we'll read the meaning of our tears, and there, sometime we'll understand."

Yes, someday we'll understand the potpourri, the mixture of events that made up our lives on earth. Though I didn't know what awaited me on the morrow, I knew the God of tomorrow was in control.

CHAPTER 25

THE HUMOROUS AND NOT SO HUMOROUS

During the winter of 1950–51, the men held regular cottage meetings in Bziza and Dar Bishtar. We hadn't intended to begin meetings in these villages just yet, but it came about in an unusual way.

Two young men, who had just been released from prison after serving a six-year sentence for committing murder, gave Wayne the Macedonian call. But first, Wayne wanted to know why they had committed murder. Their explanation was simple. "The Bible says if someone hits you on one cheek, turn the other. But if he hits that too, it doesn't say to stick out your neck. So we took care of our enemy." Evidently the judge believed that the brothers had been aggravated into committing their dastardly deed because he mitigated their sentence.

While the brothers were in prison, they enrolled in the Voice of Prophecy Bible Correspondence course. When they left prison they called Wayne to come to their home and study more with them. They invited in some of their friends, and presto! We were involved in cottage meetings in Dar Bishtar.

In the same town was another man with a different interest; he sought gainful employment. The bishop promised to get him a job at the cement factory in Shekka if he would rid the town of Adventists. So without knowing much about us, but desperate for employment, he agreed to do this.

One night Wayne and Moses were on their way home from Dar Bishtar. About a mile from the village, two men on the road hailed them. Since people were accustomed to wave down service taxis, Wayne supposed that, in the darkness, the men had mistaken his car for a service taxi. He stopped and asked what he could do for the them. Immediately the men stepped up to the car windows, shouted curses at Wayne and Moses and threatened to kill them. Wayne and Moses didn't think that sounded like fun, so they tried to reason with the men. While Wayne was talking to the older man, he noticed that the man held his hand in his coat pocket where he probably carried a concealed weapon. Wayne and Moses supposed this could be the end for them; so, during their last moments, they hoped to evangelize their antagonists. Conditions were not ideal for preaching, but Wayne seemed to be making progress with the older man. Praying for divine protection and that he would say the right words, Wayne convinced the older man that Adventists were Christians. Soon the older man was content to let Wayne and Moses go on their way if they would promise never to return to preach in Dar Bishtar.

The younger hothead, however, had wandered to the back of the car. Moses felt uncomfortable with the young man fiddling around under the bumper, so he went back to investigate. What he saw made Moses' hair stand at attention—the young man was trying to tie sticks of dynamite onto the tail pipe. Moses knew that would blow them, the car, and the environment to the utter most parts of El-Koura, so he asked him to stop. He ignored Moses request and swore at him.

THE HUMOROUS AND NOT SO HUMOROUS

Then the older man went to the back of the car and yelled at the hothead, "Come on, let's get going. The Adventists ain't so bad."

The hothead would not listen. He had come out to do a job, and he was GOING to do it. The older man became impatient with the young upstart's defiance and kicked him a wallop. That did it! The young man flew out from under the bumper, smoldering and faced his companion. While the two pushed and shoved each other and argued, Moses, seeing no need to observe their performance, jumped in the care car with Wayne. Then they sped off, leaving the two to settle their differences in the dust of the missionary's car.

On Sabbath, the most interested of the two ex-prisoners came to the Sabbath morning services at our house. Wayne told Amir about the episode on the road. Amir offered to investigate and report back the next Sabbath. In the meantime, he suggested that Wayne should not go back to his village for two weeks.

Several weeks later when Wayne resumed the Bible studies, his assailant had become disenchanted with the bishop. He had not gotten a job after all and was ready to switch his allegiance. The meetings in Dar Bishtar were over by mid-May with very few results. At the time, it hardly seemed worth the effort and risk.

Jesus commission, however, remains—preach the gospel. On this earth we may never know the results of the seeds of truth we have planted. Yet we are to sow, as the Holy Spirit waters, and God reaps the crop. Ecclesiastes 11:1 encourages us: "Cast your bread upon waters, for you shall find it after many days."

Years later we were visiting the church in Jerusalem when a young man came up to us. "You probably don't recognize me," he said, "but I was a twelve-year-old boy when you held meetings in my father's house. He was principal of the government school in those days. When I grew to manhood, I remembered the beauty of the gospel as I learned it from you. I taught my wife and two children the same wonderful message. We are members of the Adventist community here."

We were a bit choked up as we embraced this lovely family. Our bread had returned to us quadrupled! (Sometime later Assam and family immigrated to the United States.)

May in Lebanon is the beginning of the hot weather. The group in Bziza began to meet in the yard of the host's house. Besides being comfortably cooler, the white-washed wall of the old stone house served beautifully as a giant screen on which to project the Bible slides.

One night after Wayne had finished his discourse, he connected his projector to the car battery as usual—there being no electricity in Bziza as yet—and began the slide presentation. People were quietly enjoying the pictures when a drunk came up the street singing to the top of his voice disrupting the meeting. The host yelled at him to go home and keep quiet. The drunk was completely unimpressed with the request and continued to aggravate the house owner.

Then the drunk climbed up on the remains of an old Roman temple. He perched himself on the top of the wall, wobbling precariously back and forth as he croaked songs that were not at all conducive to a religious atmosphere. The house owner shouted at him again, "Have some respect! Can't you see we are studying the Bible? Now get out of here!"

The drunk knew his rights. He wouldn't be bossed around by the house owner. "Hey, thiz iz a free country, ain' it?" he shouted defiantly, "I can sing anywhere I wanna." He continued his warbling.

THE HUMOROUS AND NOT SO HUMOROUS

Now the host really lost control. He dashed into his house and came out loading his pistol. "I'll get that drunk down off the wall and quiet him for good!"

This disrupted the meeting again. No one could concentrate on the Word of Life when there was a murder about to take place. The village men pounced on the house owner, trying to disarm him. The man's sons finally snatched the gun and held their father in a chair. Then everyone settled into an uneasy peace. The drunk was gone—or so they thought. Wayne could hardly get himself back in the preaching mood, but he exhibited an outward calm and tried to remember where he'd left off. Then he noticed that the drunk had joined his audience and was sitting scrunched up against the wheel of the car. Wayne decided to wind things up in a hurry, but he didn't do it fast enough.

"OOH, thaz nice," said the drunk pointing to the pictures. "Thaz Jezuz, ain' it? Iz tha the virshun Mary?"

"Shut up, you imbecile, you, you..." the owner yelled. He had now lost his religion as well as his patience.

"He'z mad, ain' he?" the drunk remarked. He couldn't know HOW mad! Just mad enough to kill!

Wayne ended the meeting, and the people gradually drifted off to their homes. Now the drunk decided he wanted to go home with Wayne. Wayne knew I wouldn't approve of such a guest, so he tried to talk the drunk out of the idea. If he thought he was successful, he was soon to discover differently. As Wayne drove down the narrow lane to the main road, the drunk was waiting for him. "I wanna go wit you!" he yelled. Wayne stepped on the gas to go around the drunk, but quick as a cat, the drunk jumped onto the back bumper, leaned against the window and held onto the sides of the Ford for dear life. The drunk continued his serenade as Wayne carefully rounded the curves down to the valley.

MIDGE IN LEBANON

What should he do now? The seminary hadn't given Wayne a single lesson on how to get drunks off your back bumper. Henry Jeha, who was with Wayne that night, suggested, "There's a cafe in this town that is still open. I'll give the owner some money to feed him. Then he can get a ride back to his village."

The cafe manager agreed and so did the drunk. Henry and Wayne drove off rid of their baggage. No one got any merit badges for religiosity that night, but Wayne has enjoyed the humor of the incident the rest of his life.

April of 1951, the doctor ordered me to take bed rest for 10 days. I knew it was good advice, so I tried doing it. Children, however, have a way of getting us to annul the best of our intentions.

One afternoon I was resting quietly in my bed when little Germana, Ronnie's playmate, came bursting into the house and my bedroom. "Madame Olson, come quickly! Ronnie's buried under the old stone wall, and I can't get her out!"

I was so weak I could scarcely walk a few steps by myself, but with information like that, adrenalin pumped through my body, and I was up and on my way to save my daughter. As I raced to the site of the crumbling walls of the thousand year old house, I prayed and called for help. Men appeared from everywhere, and in moments they were lifting huge stones—some two feet thick—off Ronnie. Fortunately, her head hadn't been hit, but we feared her body was crushed. The stones, however, had fallen in such a miraculous way that one braced against the other thus preventing them from touching her body. Only her left ankle was pinned beneath a stone. When the stone was lifted, we knew her ankle was broken.

What should I do now? Wayne was away for three days visiting an isolated member in a village that was high in the mountains. It was impossible to contact Wayne since there was no phone in that vicinity. The village men solved my dilemma. They loaded Ronnie and me into a friend's taxi and took us to the shepherd in the next village. I hadn't known before that shepherds are excellent bone "doctors", but some are. They set the fractures of sheep by feeling, not by X-rays. When the shepherd looked at Ronnie's ankle and "felt" gently along the break, I became confident of his ability. He padded her ankle with torn strips of cloth dipped in something that made the cloth become rather stiff as it dried. Then he fastened on some padded splints and tied the leg up in such a way that she couldn't walk on it. I thanked him, paid him one dollar for his services, and went back home. I kept Ronnie in bed with me, or at least in my bedroom, until Wayne returned. Wayne wasn't convinced of the shepherd's medical skills so he took Ronnie off to the hospital to have her break examined by a REAL doctor. The set of the ankle checked out very well. The REAL doctors did nothing to change what the shepherd had done. Wayne's skepticism, however, cost us considerably more than the shepherd's fee.

For the next six weeks Ronnie enjoyed all the donkey rides and the other attention given her by the villagers. By now, we had been fully accepted by the people, and they gave Ronnie royal treatment. We tried to make sure that Ronnie didn't take advantage of this and to impress her that, hereafter, she should leave the exploration of antiquities to the archaeologists.

On Monday, June 4, Wayne went to Ras Muska for the cottage meeting at Deeb's, as usual. I was unusually tired that day and had been run ragged with diarrhea. I wasn't anxious for Wayne to leave me, but I didn't want him to neglect God's work, either. Neither Wayne nor I realized how seriously ill I really was. We had counted

MIDGE IN LEBANON

on my naturally hardy constitution to help me bounce back to normal, but after months of deteriorating health, we should have known better. Though the doctors had tried to impress us with the seriousness of my condition, I guess we both thought I was indestructible.

About 6 p.m. I got an excruciating pain in my left chest, arm, and neck. Thank God Nada and Alice Muellim were there when I passed out. They dragged me to the bed, ran to the door, and yelled for help. Many of the villagers rallied to their cry. Women came and stood over my unconscious form. They observed that my hands and feet were icy cold and blue. They filled four pans with hot water and immersed my limbs. They massaged my hands and feet, drawing the blood away from my heart. Perhaps this was the right thing to do. Someone called young Dr. Jamil from Amuin, while someone else left to look for Wayne. They thought he should be there when I died.

In less than 12 minutes Dr. Jamil arrived and gave me injections to stimulate my heart. When I came around a bit he wanted me to drink some liquor. Even in my semi-conscious condition, I knew Adventists shouldn't drink brandy, so I refused. My brain had been programmed that alcohol was a "no-no", and no doctor could persuade me to take it as a medicine. I also refused to speak Arabic with the French and Arabic speaking doctor. So five-year old Ronnalee became our translator.

No one had made contact with Wayne. When he drove in about 9 p.m. he was bewildered to see our veranda and house filled with people. Fear filled his heart as he worked his way through the crowd to the bedroom. The doctor told him that I had had a heart attack and was too ill to move. Even though I was still young, I was a prime candidate for a heart attack. First, the rheumatic fever I

THE HUMOROUS AND NOT SO HUMOROUS

had when I was seven had caused some permanent damage to my heart. This, by itself, was not considered that serious; however, my seven-month battle with dysentery and colitis had left me completely emaciated. My red and white count were extremely low. Then the doctor in Tripoli made a grave mistake that could have killed almost anyone, let alone someone in my debilitated condition. He had given me some strong, oral medication for dysentery, then, without canceling that and forgetting about my heart murmur, he gave Wayne a new medication to inject me with daily. Both the pills and the injections were very hard on the heart. Two weeks earlier the doctor had told me to get my "house in order" because he saw no way that I could survive with the complications I had developed. I can never believe he planned over-medication as a short-cut to the grave for me, but it almost turned out that way. I suspect it was an oversight on his part.

That night as I lay there in a fuzzy stupor, I really hoped it would all be over soon. I was tired of being ill. I didn't want to go to the hospital one more time for another of those miserable intravenous injections for dehydration. My veins were rebelling against punctures and every fleshy spot on my body was lumpy from intramuscular shots. I thought it was better to die. Lela would take good care of my children and things between God and me were fine, so why not just sink into eternal sleep.

Then Ronnie and David crawled upon my bed and patted my face gently. "Hurry and get well, Mommy. We love you and need you," was the essence of their pleas. That renewed my old spunk, and I determined I'd give life a good try—for their sakes—even though my erratic heartbeat tormented me.

I almost always find some humor in anything. I'm not flippant, it's just my way of coping with difficult

MIDGE IN LEBANON

situations. I saw little humor, however, in the conversation of my many visitors during the next few days. It seemed that almost every one that came to "cheer me up" honed in on the subject of death and dying. That, in itself, was not so bad, but they told horror stories of those who were thought to be dead but were actually buried alive. They told how the "dead" must have come to life in the tomb, shoved the lid off their coffins, and scratched and dug to get out of the door of their tomb. Eventually they starved to death because no one could hear them way out there in the cemetery. Their plight was not known until the tomb was opened again to put in another coffin. (There are many family tombs in Lebanon that are built like an underground cave. They are large enough for men to crawl into and place a coffin on either side of the door. Then when the next person dies, the bones are removed from the oldest coffin, and placed at the far end of the tomb. The wooden pieces of the old coffin are thrown out, making room for the newest coffin. Thus one tomb suffices for many generations. It is a practical use of space and a unique approach to "keeping the family together".)

The ladies' most graphic of cemetery stories was that of the girl down in Shekka who had recently died of typhoid. They had the wake in the house, and then, because she was young, they carried her coffin to the church with the lid off. As they carried her to the cemetery in the warmth of the March sun, she came to life, and sat up in her coffin. When she moved, the men carrying the coffin were so startled they dropped it. She fell to the ground and broke her arm, but was happy she had revived in time to stop them from burying her alive. Evidently she had only been in a coma.

For the next week I made Wayne promise again and again that he would make sure I was REAL dead before they buried me—in case I should die. I knew he would

THE HUMOROUS AND NOT SO HUMOROUS

have to bury me within 24 hours of my demise since that is the law of the land in a country where they do not embalm the corpse. He promised, but I still prayed, "Lord, please don't let me die until I get to America."

Later I could look back and laugh at the poor psychology practiced by my visitors. Thankfully they were better than Job's comforters. At least they didn't accuse me of doing evil.

I was really sorry to miss the baptism on Sabbath June 9, and Farris and Laurice's wedding the next day, but I was too weak to move from my bed.

The doctor came to the house daily to give me a vitamin shot and make sure I swallowed my charcoal pills. Those pills were so large they would have made a horse balk, but I finally got the knack of downing them. My diet was rather tiresome too—goat meat and yogurt, scraped apple, and boiled rice.

After two weeks I was strong enough to ride with the family to the camp meeting in Beirut. Laura Appel, the division president's wife, looked after me and the children. My body ached from staying in bed; she massaged me which helped me sleep. I was down to 93 pounds; she urged me to take "just one more bite". She bathed and powdered me and kept the children fed, clean, and happy. She was an angel of mercy.

By the time I left Appel's house in Beirut, I was feeling much better. My sense of humor had returned, even though I still wasn't ready to take on the world. I wasn't ready for what we soon would face back home, either.

CHAPTER 26

SHAKING DUST

We thought we had seen a lot of fierce opposition to the preaching of the gospel, but in no way could we have anticipated the violence we would face when we started our evangelistic effort in Amuin during the summer of 1951. Since a number of people had requested that we hold a series of meetings in this town, we laid plans accordingly. Amuin was a nice town of educated people. It should have been a safe place too. The government center for the district of El-Koura, the sheriff's office, the police station, and courthouse were there.

In April, Michael Kebbas moved to Amuin where he aroused an interest in the gospel by holding children's meetings. This strategy had always worked well in other places. The children enjoyed the stories and songs they learned from Michael and carried the message home. Thus, they unwittingly tantalized the adults into attending our meetings.

We rented a room where we could meet quietly and unobtrusively in a house set back about 50 yards from the street. Michael used the room for the children's meetings; we would use the flat roof top for the evangelistic meetings. We built a cement block banister around the edge of the roof to make it safer for the people. The banister wasn't strong, but it delineated the periphery of the roof. We moved our platform to the roof, set up chairs, and installed lights. When we began our

MIDGE IN LEBANON

meetings on Tuesday night, July 3, we had no idea that enemies had schemed to harm us.

I went with Wayne and Moses to the meeting that first night. I shouldn't have gone because Dr. Jamil had ordered me to stay in bed and avoid all stress. But I felt responsible to be there. Moses was going to have to do double duty as it was—lead the song service and translate. Farris Bishi, who had translated for Wayne in Bishmizeen, had moved to Sudan with his bride to start work there. Wayne had tried to get an organist to take my place, but no one was available. I knew it was hard for Moses to lead a song service without an instrumental back-up, so I forced myself from bed, dressed, and went to the meeting.

We parked our car off the street behind some houses and walked through an alley to the meeting place. Wayne carried me up the stone steps to the roof since I was too weak to walk. I don't know how I thought I'd have the energy to peddle the pump organ, but I didn't seem to think too clearly those days.

About 150 people attended our first meeting despite the warning of the clergy and their cohorts. There was some noise below us that night, but up on the roof we were able to ignore it. The stones they threw onto the roof were harder to ignore, but no one was hit. Then a loud impact on the edge of the banister, followed almost instantaneously by a deafening explosion, scared us half to death. A pipe bomb the foe intended should land on the roof fell short, nicked the top cement block of the banister, and plummeted to the rock quarry below on the east side of the house. The explosion shook the house, but no one was hurt. It scared the neighbor's donkey through the fence. The owner found him two days later, but I don't know if his hearing was ever restored.

SHAKING DUST

Thursday night was our second meeting. Ronnie begged to go with us and, for whatever reason, we foolishly took her along.

When we arrived, men were milling about the site shouting threats. Michael warned Wayne, "You'd better go for the gendarmes right away. There's going to be BIG trouble here tonight." Michael was very perceptive, anticipating what would happen before it began. When he had a conviction, we had learned to listen.

Wayne went to the police station immediately, but there was no one there. We suspected this had been planned. Wayne drove around town looking for help but no police were on the streets, either. In the meantime, Moses and I began the song service, while Michael stood at the top of the steps carefully scanning the people as they entered.

Little Ronnie sat on a front chair singing lustily in Arabic. I smiled as I watched her—she was as much Arab as any Lebanese child. At that peaceful moment I had no idea that shortly all of us on the roof would look into the face of death.

I don't remember what we were singing when the rabble arrived, but I remember what happened next with video re-run clarity. Michael tried to persuade the ruffians to leave, but they shoved him aside and walked onto the roof. One of the toughs demanded that Wayne Olson come to him. When he discovered Wayne was gone, he flew into a rage, screaming curses and obscenities. Then he darted over to the owner of the house. "If I can't kill Olson, I'll get you! You traitor! You dog! Renting property to infidels!" (In the book of Acts it tells this is what happened to Jason at Thessolonica when the Jews couldn't get to Paul.) Then he grabbed the unsuspecting owner by his shirt collar, whipped out his knife, and jabbed for his throat. Just before the knife made contact, the owner's 21-year-old daughter made a leaping jump, caught the assailant's arm, and forced the knife to slip off to the side. Then the assailant's accomplices grabbed and held the young lady.

The attacker went after the owner a second time. Quick as a cat, Michael pounced on the man and threw him off balance. In the struggle the man dropped his knife, the steel blade shattering to bits as it hit the cement roof. The attacker was rabid with anger, but Michael held him tight until the owner's sons relieved him. Then others entered the fracas and things went from bad to worse. In moments the fight on the roof was out of control. Since they couldn't find Wayne, they determined to get Michael, Moses, and me. To save Ronnie's life, I told her to hide behind the organ, and if the men came that way, to crawl under the platform. I told her to stay there until all was quiet, and then, if she couldn't find me, she should go down stairs to the lady of the house. The lady would tell her what to do next. Ronnie understood and obeyed immediately.

A mobster yelled, "EVERYONE, leave immediately or you will be killed."

The people were paralyzed with fear and sat immobile. They would have fled as the evil men advised them, but they couldn't. The mob was so frenzied they didn't seem to realize that they were blocking the only entrance/exit stair case. When their orders weren't obeyed, the villains picked up the empty chairs in the last two rows and hurled them into the crowd. Then a most spectacular miracle took place in the sight of everyone. As a chair flew above the audience, it stayed suspended in the air, held by an invisible hand, until the person underneath it escaped. The chair would then drop straight down. It happened again and again. This amazed and awed us. The phenomenon checked the rage of the mob temporarily.

Our crowd panicked and ran away from the mob toward the east side of the roof. I worried as I saw the terrorized people crushing one another in an ever tightening pack closer and closer to the edge of the roof. What if the feeble cement block banister gave way? The thought was horrifying—people would plunge two stories down into the stone quarry below.

Then God prodded me into action. "Go over and talk to the nicely dressed man standing by the top of the stairs with his arms folded," someone seemed to say.

I never questioned that directive for a moment. I had no idea who the man was nor what I would say. When I reached him I heard myself saying, "You are a lawyer and in charge of this mob. If anyone gets hurt here tonight, you will be held responsible. There are many witnesses here that know you."

"Ha, ha!" he laughed heinously. "No one can touch me. The bishop and I have it all figured out. If there is a murder, the accused will go to jail for only a few weeks. I am the only witness that will be admitted into court, and we will buy off the judge, if I have to. You don't have a chance!"

"Oh, yes, we do," I countered. "We have a bona-fide permit now…"

"I know. It's filed here in Amuin, but we will destroy that tomorrow."

"Then did you know that the permit on file here in Amuin is only a copy? We have other copies in the government offices of Tripoli and Beirut. We also have copies in our mission and division vaults. You won't be able to destroy all of the them. We've taken plenty of precaution. Besides, most of the people in town are not in league with you. Further, you are dealing with Syrian and American citizens, not just Lebanese. If anyone is hurt or killed, you will have a lot more people to answer to than your local authorities. As a lawyer, you ought to consider these ramifications before you proceed further. None of your mobsters, and especially you, will get off easy. God is with us. You will pay the full penalty for your crimes."

I was shocked by my eloquence. The words were coming out of my mouth, but not from my brain. How could this happen?

How could I say he was a lawyer and the leader of the mob? I didn't know that; I'd never seen the man before. By nature I am a coward. In this type of situation I would have hid in the crowd rather than take the initiative. But tonight was different. I felt that I was acting under Divine inspiration.

The man was struck speechless by my indictment. I surprised myself by continuing. "We know your Lebanese laws and we insist upon our rights to religious freedom. How would the story of your intolerance look in an American journal? Worse! How does this violence in the name of Christianity appear in the eyes of a Holy God? God is HERE watching over us. You can't fight Him!"

The lawyer was visibly shaken. "Wh—what shall I do?" he asked through ashen lips in a tremulous voice.

"Call off the attack. Get all your buddies off the roof immediately before someone gets hurt."

I wasn't even surprised when he followed my directive and yelled for everyone to leave. I felt God had taken charge and was using my mouth.

At first the men were slow to respond to the lawyer's command. Then he yelled, "If you guys don't leave right now, you'll rot in jail. These folks have legal permits and their governments will be on our backs—not to mention the help they're getting from God."

The mob scrambled for the stairs, hoping that no one would remember them and their part in the fracas.

We were all deeply shaken after the mob left. I collapsed into a chair and called Ronnie to come out from behind the organ.

"Are the bad men gone, Mommy?" Ronnie asked. I assured her that they were, and that they wouldn't be back again that night.

So much for my doctor's orders to avoid stress. Now I knew STRESS!!

When Wayne got back to the roof, all of the excitement was over. The chairs were set up again, and the people were attempting to sing. Their quavering voices, however, reflected the affect of their horrifying experience. Since it was late, Wayne launched right into his sermon. He didn't know until after the meeting was over what had transpired in his absence.

The next day Wayne filed charges against three of the leaders. When the case came to court, all of the witnesses and the accused were present. The judge read the accusations, then turned to Wayne for affirmation. Wayne acknowledged the facts as stated were true, but said he didn't want to press the charges.

"But they are guilty!" the judge exclaimed. (He could have added "with intent to kill" but he didn't.) "What do you think I should do with them?"

"Nothing. I really don't want any adversity to come to them. I just want peace," Wayne added.

"All right," the judge answered shaking his head in disbelief. "You may drop the charges, but public justice must still be executed. I therefore fine the accused 15

MIDGE IN LEBANON

Lebanese lira each, and their offense of causing a public disturbance will go on their permanent record."

The men appreciated Wayne's spirit and respected him for his benevolence. They also learned that they couldn't flaunt the law and get by with it and that those religious leaders who claimed unlimited power, didn't really have it, after all. This knowledge subdued the defendants and other potential trouble makers. There remained, however, a few rascals who kept up the harassment.

The sheriff insisted that from now on we meet inside the building since it was quite impossible to protect us on an open roof top at night.

Wayne, Moses, and Michael carried the chairs down into the room and stored the platform and lights. They nailed wire mesh over the windows to prevent the large stones from entering the house. Then, since there was still a threat that someone would shoot Wayne and Moses, the men planned to stand between two windows while speaking so that they would be out of the line of fire. We were now prepared to continue the meetings on a smaller scale. We weren't ready to shake the dust from our feet and give up on Amuin—not yet.

Sunday night, July 8, we went to Amuin as usual, parked the car behind some houses, and started walking through the alley to the house. On the way, we were bombarded with stones thrown by people who were hiding behind buildings. I had to steel myself against the urge to run. I prayed for courage and was able to walk sedately, purposefully into the meeting room. Miraculously, the stones landed on either side of us or behind us. Those throwing the stones seemingly had no control over the missiles once they left their hands. Some mysterious hand guided the stones away from all of us who went to the meeting that night. The two gendarmes who were there to protect us, however, ran for the safety of a shed. They didn't get hit, either—they locked themselves in a stone building for protection. A lot of help they were!!

Elder Appel, the division president, was quite concerned over what was happening to us in the north. Those in the peaceful Beirut area could hardly believe that we were facing such violence only 50 miles away. On Tuesday evening, George and Laura Appel and another carload of mission officers from Beirut came up to Amuin to investigate.

Wherever the agitators were hiding, they must have seen the two cars with Beirut license tags drive up. The noise and stone throwing stopped abruptly. They remained quiet all through the meeting, yet there was a tenseness in the air. We learned later that the trouble makers were busy trying to figure out who the people from Beirut were. They suspected they were secret agents dressed like business men and feared that they had a bevy of back-up men hidden somewhere. So the "bad boys" vanished into the darkness fearing the consequences if they got caught or reported. After all, their "big boys" had been humbled by the government, and it was only Wayne's mercy that had saved them from further punishment.

We enjoyed conducting a peaceful meeting that night and wished that the brethren from Beirut would make their visitations a regular practice. When the meeting was over, the mission folks got in their car and left. They had seen nothing disturbing or dangerous—just a half dozen stones. The Appels stayed and talked with our staff awhile. Then we left for home just ahead of them.

Five minutes after we got home there was frantic knocking at our door. "Are you folks all right?" Elder Appel called, sounding very frightened.

"We surely are. That was the best meeting we've had in Amui…"

Elder Appel interrupted, "We are pretty much shaken. When we drove through the town, someone rolled huge stones off a roof that hung over the road. They landed on the back end of our car crushing big dents into the trunk."

We went out to see his car. We were astonished to see the extent of the damage. It would cost a lot to repair the dents.

"This is terrible!" Elder Appel exclaimed. "Nothing like this ever happened to us during all the years we spent in China. I think you should shake the dust from your feet and leave Amuin. Your persecutors are mean, relentless men. Since they do their dirty work in the cover of darkness, they can keep this nonsense going forever."

We knew Elder Appel was right, and we should have taken his advice then. But we weren't ready to give in to the devil's forces.

Thursday night we passed through another barrage of stones on our way to the meeting house. Mercifully, divine intervention sheltered us again. During the meeting, they continued to throw stones and make noise. Wayne and Moses stood with their backs to the stone wall between the windows. Even then, one stone hit the iron bar on the window so forcefully that it shattered the stone. The chips flew through the wire mesh and landed on us. We managed to get through the meeting, but now we needed to get home.

When Moses, Wayne, and I got into the car, a strange sensation came over me. "Wayne," I said, "we must go home through Bishmizeen."

"What!" Wayne exclaimed. "It's farther that way. Gas is too expensive to go extra miles."

"I know," I sighed, "but I have this strong conviction that we must take the long way home."

"Yes! I also feel that we should go via Bishmizeen," Moses concurred.

"Well, all right," Wayne agreed reluctantly, as he turned the car around and headed for Bishmizeen. We got home safely.

The next day Wayne went to the police station and reminded them that they neglected to send protection for us the previous night. The sergeant offered a feeble excuse and promised that he would have a force to protect us from then on —but only once a week. So Wayne agreed to hold only Sunday night meetings.

Sunday night, July 15, we walked through another volley of stones. This time one young man got hit on the head. He had to go to the doctor and have six stitches taken to close the gap. The meeting finished without further incident, and we were ready to go home again. Again I received a strong conviction. "Wayne, this time I really feel that we should take the short way home."

"I was just going to say the same thing," Moses added.

"'That's the way I prefer anyway," Wayne laughed, "so it's unanimous."

As we reached home Wayne remarked, "See, there was nothing dangerous about taking the short way home, now was there?"

I didn't answer. I believed my strong impressions were from God, but how could I convince anyone of that?

The next Sunday night, there were no police on hand as they had promised. Many stones were thrown, and there was much disturbance. I looked out through a chicken-wire covered window of the meeting house and commented, "A person could bring in a rock crushing machine and set up business here. Stones are plentiful and handy."

None of us was humored by my satirical remark; things were far too serious.

Once more we were in the car, ready to start for home. Jokingly Wayne asked, "Well, clairvoyant companions, which way home tonight?"

Without a moment's hesitation, Moses and I said simultaneously, "The long way."

The next day I began to question my sanity. We always got home safely, so why were Moses and I so paranoid? We had no sound reason for our strong impressions. A few days later we got the answer.

It was late, about 10 p.m., when an interloper appeared at our door. Wayne knew he was one who "bumped people off" for a fee. We felt a little apprehensive admitting a person with such an infamous occupation into our home. None the less, he was there, and we were at his mercy.

"What can we do for you?" Wayne asked.

I thought that was a stupid question. My concern was "What are you planning to do to us?" But I was too afraid to ask.

We chit-chatted a bit, and then the man got down to business. "I know who your enemies are," he said. "I have come here to offer protective services."

"And how do you propose to do that?" Wayne inquired.

SHAKING DUST

"You hire me, and I will take your enemies out to coffee and persuade them that you are good people. Then they'll leave you alone," the man explained.

"And suppose they won't listen to you?"

"I'll share with them some of the money you give me. If they're still contrary, this baby helps them decide to cooperate," he replied as he pulled out his 45 caliber, Belgium-made, 14-shot automatic pistol.

"Well, friend, (I wouldn't have used that term, either. I didn't feel that chummy with our visitor.) we're in the business of saving souls, not taking lives. We work for God and, therefore, we depend upon Him to protect us. Thanks, anyway."

"Talking about protection, I want to ask you something. Honestly, how did you know that the last three nights there were men lying in wait on the road to kill you as you drove home."

"WHAT?" Wayne and I asked wide eyed.

"Yeah," the man said. "One night they laid on the short way, and you went through Bishmizeen. The next night the three of them rolled stones across the road to Bishmizeen, and you went home the short way. Then the last night they waited on the short way, and you went the long way. How did you know where they were? Who was your informant?"

"Maybe it was God," Wayne said reverently. "What do the men who waited for us on the road think?"

"Well, at first they thought that they were being betrayed by other villagers—your friends. But now they aren't sure. The three of them always stayed together because none of them wanted to risk being alone on the road. You know—if they'd miss, maybe you would have a gun and get them. So the three always went together. When you eluded them the third time, they got superstitious. Now none of them will lay for you on the road anymore. They think bad luck will come to them if they try again. Three times and out. So they are out." The man laughed artificially.

"Let me just explain our reason for changing our routes to get home," Wayne said. "My wife and Moses got impressions that we should go home as we went those three nights. Do you think that God might have had a hand in it?"

"I do," the man said solemnly, "and I believe you are good people. I guess the likes of you don't need my protection—not when you've got His."

Wayne read from the Bible to the man and prayed with him. It made a profound impression upon him, and he left with tears in his eyes. We hoped that he would repent like the thief on the cross and be saved. We don't know what became of our night visitor. We never saw him again.

On August 2, just a month after our meetings began, Wayne talked with the khaimakam. The two agreed that it would be best to suspend public meetings in Amuin indefinitely. We would continue the private Bible studies in homes.

Sunday afternoon, August 12, Wayne and a friend gave a Bible study to a family on the very outskirts of Amuin. As they walked back down the dusty lane to the main road and our car, two monks and Lail stepped out of a taxi and confronted them. "Now we've got you," Lail snarled. "You're way out here alone—no one to witness anything—we could kill you."

Our friend caught a glimpse of knives and realized there was danger.

"Why would you want to kill us? Don't you know that where the blood of one martyr is shed, many more converts spring up to take his place? We are only preaching the Word of God," Wayne explained.

"Don't talk to us about the Word of God! We are following in the traditions of Christ and the apostles. Your Bible is different from ours. It should be destroyed!" Lail grabbed Wayne's Bible and threw it forcefully to the ground, ripping away the binding and tearing pages.

They continued to shout obscenities and death threats. Wayne and our friend thought they may very well end up martyrs out there on the edge of nowhere. They prayed for God to send help quickly.

Just when things had reached the point where the frenzied three were ready to act more violently, a car came screeching to a stop beside them. Three men popped out and hit the ground yelling, "Don't touch Olson and the other guy or you're in for it!"

"Yeah! You cursed crows—dressed in black like the core of your hearts!" the second man added. "Now get out of here and don't you (expletives) ever come back."

The language was more abusive than that, but it should not be put in print. The "angels" God sent to rescue His messengers bore little resemblance to the celestial beings either in language or deportment, but their presence was effective, nonetheless.

Lail and the monks fled the scene. Wayne and our friend thanked the three men for helping them, but got little explanation as to the reason for their appearance. Sometime later Wayne learned that the motive of the three men who came to their rescue was very little better than that of the monks and Lail. Others in the village revealed this story:

Early in the afternoon the two monks and Lail sat in a coffee shop discussing their plans to scare/kill Wayne to rid the village of Adventists. They had learned that Wayne and our friend were going to the edge of the village to study the Bible with the Kameel family. This secluded area would be the ideal spot to scare/beat up/or do whatever to Wayne. There would be no witnesses.

Wayne's rescuers were in the same coffee shop and overheard the discussion. The three of them were enemies of Lail since he had cheated them in a business deal. When they heard Lail plotting with the monks against the Adventists, they decided that this was a perfect set-up for them to take their revenge. They could beat up Lail while pretending to protect Wayne. Their plan had been only partially successful, however. Though they arrived in time to save the Adventists, they didn't get the chance to take revenge. The monks and Lail fled too soon. This incident caused Lail to back off from us for a few weeks, but he hadn't learned his lesson yet.

On Sunday afternoon, August 26, Michael was conducting the children's meeting as usual. The room was filled with happy children singing lustily when suddenly a burly figure darkened the door. Michael looked up and saw Lail standing there, wielding his knife menacingly. Lail was a bit muddled since he had just been given a few beers by our adversaries.

"Stop fillin' dose chilern of da true shursh with your hear-sy!" Lail barked as he started down the aisle toward Michael.

Fortunately Michael was stronger and more agile than Lail. Michael picked up one of the heavy wooden chairs and lunged for Lail. Holding the chair at arm's length between them, Michael pushed Lail toward the door. The two were still struggling when neighbors arrived and joined the fracas on Michael's side. The frightened children had scrambled over the chairs or

SHAKING DUST

jumped from the windows to the street and told people what Lail was doing. Then angry mothers sprinted down the road to the meeting place, ready to rip Mr. Lail apart. Mother hens are more than feisty when it comes to protecting their chicks, as Lail summarily learned. The trouble maker barely escaped with his clothes intact. The parents then instigated such an anti-Lail campaign that it was hardly safe for the man to remain in town. His enmity to us had known no bounds; now the tables were turned toward him.

That took care of Lail. We were relieved never to see or hear from him again. He had been a participant in the persecution from its inception. We knew he was also the one who stole our song books.

In the midst of the summer's turmoil, some of our good friends in Amuin became ill. I couldn't be of much help to this family, however, because I was still in and out of both my bed and the hospital. Subsisting on bland food and vitamin injections didn't build up my energy level much, and the conditions in Amuin only added to my stress.

One day I was feeling better, so I went over to Amuin with Wayne. I cleaned our friends' house and cooked some food for them while Wayne and Michael made house calls. Toward evening Wayne and Michael came by the house to pick me up. Just at that moment, the communist son of Mrs. Emil, the house owner, entered the scene.

Our friends had rented the right wing of Emil's house for the summer. The Emil family occupied the left wing of the house. Between the two wings was a common living room of gigantic proportions. At either end of the living room were doors that led outside—one to the steps of the front door and the path that went through the terraces down the steep hill to the road, and the other door led to the back yard where the kitchen and bath were housed in a separate building. Both wings had side doors that opened into the common living room and one that led from their quarters to the outside.

Wayne stayed in the car while Michael ran up to the common living room door and called me. The half-drunk communist son poked his head out of his part of the house and yelled, "Iz Mizter O'zon here? I wanna kill tha' Americani!"

"No," Michael answered. "He's not here; his wife is."

"Where! Where?" he cried. "I'll kill tha' Americani!"

He grabbed his stick and started out of the house to find me. If he couldn't get Wayne, I would do as a substitute. I was ignorant of his plans, however, as I came from the kitchen into the living room with a bowl of soup for our friends. Michael and the Commie saw me at the same time. Michael screamed in English. "Get out of here, Midge. Run around the house and down the terrace steps to the car."

At the same instant the Commie was shrieking in Arabic, "I'll kill you Americani."

I took a quick glance at the deranged man and was off. The soup splashed out as I plopped the bowl down on the kitchen counter on my way around the outside of the left wing. The man ducked from the living room back into his side of the house to catch me as I ran past their side door. Through the window I saw the man headed for his door, and I knew we would meet head-on. The realization struck me that I was about to be killed!

At the last moment, the man's grown sister jumped in front of him, stopping him short. In his rage he beat her with the stick and broke her arm. Her shrieks rent the air as she fell to the floor writhing in pain. Then the wild one slipped back into the living room to meet me as I came through the back door headed for the front steps that lead down the terraces to the road.

Again we were about to meet. Michael grabbed him and yelled out orders to me, "Go back the other way."

I ran back the other way while Michael struggled with my foe, trying to keep him from getting at me. Fortunately, the contender was no match for Michael who had developed his muscles working on his father's farm in Syria. When Michael got our antagonist away from the front door, he called directions to me again, "Run through the living room now, out the front door, and down the steps to the car. HURRY!"

I obeyed and, believe me, I hurried! I didn't bother with the steps. I simply jumped down the three-foot terraces, concealing myself as best I could under the grape arbor. I was completely out of breath by the time I reached the car, opened the door, and collapsed on the front seat beside Wayne.

The next minute Michael yanked open the back door and jumped in. "Hurry, Wayne, get out of here!"

"Why?" Wayne wanted to know.

"Mrs. Emil's son is coming to kill you folks. He's stumbling down the terrace steps now," Michael shouted. "MOVE!"

"NO," Wayne argued, "I'll just wait here and reason with him."

"You can't! He's drunk and crazy as a loon. GO, I say! GO NOW!" Michael shouted.

Wayne was still not convinced. Slowly he started the engine and put the car in gear. I stretched my foot across the transmission hump, kicked his foot off the clutch and pressed on the gas peddle. We lurched forward just as the Commie reached our car. He yelled for us to stop so he could kill us. But I kept my foot in place. I wasn't about to cooperate with him.

The man yanked on Michael's door but it was locked. The car gained momentum just as the Communist lifted his stick and hit at the car. He was only able to strike a glancing blow on our trunk as we spun away. Even so, when we got home and examined the damage, I was glad the big dent was on our trunk instead of my head. Once again we had escaped.

September came, and still the opposition persisted. They even began making life difficult for our friends. So some of the interested families and Michael moved to Bishmizeen. We had lived three months on the edge of life, and still we saw no mellowing attitude in Amuin. Six weeks earlier, Elder Appel had advised us to leave the town. The continuing violent opposition created an environment so threatening that the people who sincerely wanted to study the Bible would no longer come to the meetings. The instigators of the trouble, though only a dozen in number, were able to make life miserable for us and their fellow towns people. Therefore, we concluded that it would be best to discontinue the public meetings and study privately with the interested ones in their homes. Now the time had come when we were willing to shake the dust from our feet, and we did.

CHAPTER 27

COPING WITH DEATH

During the years of 1950–51 I was seriously ill with bouts of dysentery and ulcerative colitis. I seemed to get a little worse after each attack. I became so weak I could hardly put one foot in front of the other. Twenty bowel movements daily, mostly of pus and blood, brought my weight down to 90 pounds. My June 4, 1951 heart attack and the stress-filled encounters in Amuin only added to my misery. The doctors told me that I could not live long in that condition. Honestly, by then, I didn't care to live, either. I had to enter the hospital at least once a month to be fed intravenously. I dreaded that because it had become increasingly difficult to find a usable vein. I was not yet 30 years old but had begun hoping I would die soon, not morosely nor from self-pity. I had lived 28 exciting, marvelous years and thought I had probably fulfilled my life's assignment. I just didn't want the process to drag on any longer.

Wayne wasn't willing to give up—not yet. He heard about Dr. Khayat, a Lebanese intestinal specialist on leave from Mayo Brothers Clinic, and took me to Beirut to see him. After numerous tests, Dr. Khayat conceded that my case was almost hopeless, but agreed to take me as a patient anyway. He kept me on the goat meat-yogurt-rice-apple diet and gave me weekly injections to "help me gain weight." Evidently it helped. By November, I had gained a little weight and strength. I read the verses in Psalms 118: 17 and 18 (NIV), and believed it had been written just for me: "I shall not die but live, and recount the deeds of the Lord. The Lord has chastened me sorely, but has not given me over to death."

Dr. Khayat advised us to get a complete change of scenery and get away from the stress of our work in North Lebanon. So we packed up the children and went to Iraq. It was an exciting vacation. We saw old Ninevah, Korsabad, Babylon, Ur of the Chaldees, and many other historical and Biblical sites. We returned the last of November, refreshed and anxious to get back to work.

I was just getting into the mood for Christmas when word reached us that little Akram Razzouk had died. Akram was our special Bible student from Afesdik. It had been a real thrill to study with the folks in Afesdik the previous winter (1950–51). They were highly intelligent, motivated, family-oriented people. We met in the home of Mr. Melki, a leading citizen. Young Edmund Melki scoured the town to bring in the audience. Among those he persuaded to attend was Yacoub and Mona Razzouk, and their son, Akram. Every Sunday morning we coaxed our Ford up the muddy lane to Afesdik. And every Sunday morning, Venice Simaan, Melkis, and Razzouks were there waiting. Seven-year old Akram always sat on the front row as close to Wayne as possible. It was amazing how much of the message the lad absorbed. It was difficult to ascertain if Akram's parents were as enthusiastic about Adventism as he was. One day Akram confided to me, "I'm going to be a preacher like Mr. Olson." I expected he would, too.

When summer came, we discontinued our Sunday morning meetings in Afesdik and put our energies into the effort in Amuin. Occasionally Yacoub would bring his family over to Farhazier on Sabbath mornings. It

COPING WITH DEATH

was a three mile hike, so Yacoub made it easier for his little boys, Akram, Naji, and Nabil, by giving them turns riding the donkey. The children's Sabbath School was always more fun when the Razzouk boys were there. They were enthusiastic participators.

The Razzouks didn't have much of this world's goods. They were just honest folks struggling to make a living on their small farm and notions shop. Their home was simple and sparsely furnished, but the boys must have felt rich in their atmosphere of love.

Then one day in late summer, their security was threatened. Yacoub was up on the roof of their old house, removing the clay covering so that he could replace it with a cement roof. Suddenly he felt a weakness in his right hand which then traveled down his side. He felt no pain but knew something serious was wrong. He managed to get down from the roof and into bed. Each succeeding day his condition worsened. Finally, he borrowed money and went to a doctor. He took the medicine but to no avail. Next Yacoub was transferred to the American University Hospital of Beirut where he saw a bevy of neurologists. The specialists in Beirut knew that the blood wasn't moving through Yacoub's brain right, but they had no solutions, either. A week passed and Yacoub's condition continued to deteriorate. By the second Sabbath he was comatose, his jaw was disengaged, and his right side shook with seizures. The doctors moved him to a hospital in Tripoli to die. A relative went up to Afesdik to prepare the tomb for burial.

Yacoub's mother wanted the family to pray to the saints, but Mona couldn't do that since she had learned from the Bible that she should approach God directly. So Mona prayed and promised God that if Yacoub recovered, she would no longer fight the gospel as taught by the Adventists.

Wayne went to the hospital to visit Yacoub on Sabbath evening. Yacoub's appearance was most grotesque. Dr. Nakhli manipulated Yacoub's jaw to get it back into place, but Yacoub was dying. Wayne prayed that God would grant Yacoub a miracle.

After Wayne left, a partial miracle occurred. Yacoub began to improve almost immediately—he became fully conscious, sat up, and stopped seizing. One of the visitors in the room, rushed up to the village and rang the church bell. Mona gasped when she heard the bell toll; she feared Yacoub had died. (The church bell is always rung when there is a death in the village, but it is also rung for happy occasions.)

A few days later, the villagers and the family rejoiced as Yacoub returned home. It took two more years until he completely recovered from his paralysis, however.

At first Mona was faithful in keeping her vow to study the Bible and do what she learned. But then, she got too busy with other things. Akram reminded his mother to read the Bible and go to the meetings, but Mona couldn't seem to find time for religious matters.

The fall olive picking season was upon them. Mona and the children did most of the work because Yacoub was still partially paralyzed. As Akram drove the donkey carrying the last of the olives home, he got wet and chilled in the late November rain and developed a serious case of pneumonia. The village priest came to pray for him, but Akram objected. "Don't have the priest pray for me. Call Mr. Olson. Last summer Papa got better when Pastor prayed for him."

COPING WITH DEATH

During Akram's last painful minutes he gasped, "If I don't get well, you folks become Adventists, and I'll see you in heaven." Then Akram died.

It was one of the saddest days of my life when I attended his funeral on December 4, 1951. Though Yacoub and I had both gone through the dark valley earlier, it was Akram's death with which we must cope. It wasn't easy. He would have become a minister for God. Or had Akram already done his witnessing?

All of the Razzouk family and some of the Simaan and Melki families joined the church. Mona* was baptized on May 16, 1953, along with Venice Simaan and four of the Jeha family. At the time Mona was baptized she was pregnant with another child. When the boy was born, she called him Akram. "Because," she said, "the first Akram taught me to be faithful. I want this Akram, who was baptized before his birth, to be as faithful as his brother." (See Appendix)

We await the day when the two Akrams will meet in heaven.

*Yacoub and the boys were baptized at various times later.

CHAPTER 28

THE LEAST OF HIS LITTLE ONES

It was hard for me to put much enthusiasm into Christmas preparations the year we lost Akram. Yet I knew I should plan Christmas for my own children. So I forced myself to get busy and make Christmas gifts for them.

Late at night, when the children were sleeping, Wayne and I made a two-story doll house out of a wooden apple box for Ronnalee. We made partitions to create a bathroom and two bedrooms upstairs, and a living room, dining room and kitchen down stairs. I painted each room a different color, made curtains for the windows, crocheted little rugs for the floors, and cut material for covers for the little wooden beds. We were able to make most of the furniture out of spools and thin slabs of wood. I purchased some little plastic dolls and special furnishings in a toy store—stove, refrigerator, sewing and washing machines.

For David we made a filling station/garage with a ramp going up to a car park on the second floor. This too was made in an apple box. The gas pump was an empty metal adhesive tape spool that we bent and painted. With a hose attached, it looked quite real. We painted the garage red and white. Above the leather-hinged door we painted the words "David's Filling Station and Garage". Then we purchased some Dinky (English brand name) cars and a wrecker. The week before Christmas we had everything ready and hidden away.

MIDGE IN LEBANON

Holidays always made me nostalgic for my home in South Dakota and my German-Danish parents who had special traditions for every festival. One particularly dreary afternoon a few days before Christmas the children and I were holed up in the living room—the only warm room in the house. Our fuel oil space heater was capable of flushing the chill from only one room. As I watched 4-year-old David and 6-year-old Ronnalee playing on the carpet, I decided I should start some family traditions of my own. So, I put some records on the stereo and we sang Christmas carols. I told them the Christmas story, and soon we all had the Christmas spirit.

Our next plan was to make Christmas cookies for the poor children of the neighborhood. In the kitchen we were warmed by the oven and the thoughts of our project. With cookie cutters we pressed Christmas trees, angels, and stars out of soft dough.

We had just finished our creations of love when we heard a knock at the door. I opened it. A Bedouin lady stood outside with a tiny baby wrapped in a shawl. "Please," she said, "give me some sugar knotted in a cloth for my baby to suck. He is just newborn and it will stimulate his digestion."

I didn't argue with her logic. I pulled her out of the cold wind into my warm, good-smelling kitchen. She laid her baby on the kitchen table and unwrapped him from the shawl, exposing his unwashed naked little body. While I recovered from the shock that this baby really was only a few hours old, the mother told me her story.

Her tribe had just moved from the summer pastures in the higher elevations of our mountain. She had known that her baby was due soon, so she had gone to gather sticks and wood before its arrival. She'd felt well when

THE LEAST OF HIS LITTLE ONES

she left her tent that morning, but several miles from her camp, labor began.

Quickly she scanned the territory for shelter. The closest building was a 1,000-year-old church, and she got protection from the wind beside its crumbling walls. There she'd delivered this boy, her second child, by herself. She had tied the cord with strips of cloth from her skirt and cut the cord by hitting one stone against another.

After she had rested for a short time, she had walked the short distance into our village. She'd ambled down our street, wondering which house would receive her and grant her a little sugar and relief from the cold. She knew her class of people, the Bedouin herdsmen, were considered the least among the people of the Middle East. They were the outcasts.

This mother had found herself in front of our house and felt impressed to knock. Had God sent her to us so we could practice the gift of giving? I was humbled that we should be given the privilege to help her.

I suggested that we heat some water and give the baby his first bath. "No," she answered, "that is not our way. It will give him a cold. If you wish, you may warm a little olive oil, and I will cleanse him with that."

In moments the olive oil was ready. I handed the mother cotton sponges and towels, and we watched her lovingly care for her infant. My children stood in awe of this tiny bundle. Ronnie counted his little pink toes, while David examined fingers that were smaller than his. Gently they touched his soft cheeks and baby hair.

When the olive oil cleansing was completed, the baby fell asleep in the warmth of my kitchen. Tenderly the mother swaddled him in her old shawl, thanked me, and stood to leave.

MIDGE IN LEBANON

"Wait," I said. "Let me give you some clothes for your baby. It's three miles back to your camp, and the little fellow will get too cold before you reach your tent. I'm sure I still have a few of my children's baby clothes."

Tears fell from her soft, brown eyes onto tanned cheeks. She was young and beautiful, but she lived in meager, harsh circumstances—so different from mine. We were strangers from different worlds. Hers would never change.

I put my arm around her. I felt a kinship with this child of God and wanted to share with her the hope of eternal salvation. "We are sisters," I said. "We have the same Father." She nodded and smiled, touched that I should put myself in her class.

As I wiped my own eyes, I seated her at my table. I gave her cheese, bread, fruit, and hot tea. The children shared some of their cookies with her while I scrounged in my old trunk.

David and Ronnalee were thrilled to share their outgrown garments with this baby. They watched with pleasure as I dressed him in a cotton shirt, diapers, a nightie, and a faded sweater and cap. Then the mother swaddled her infant in her old shawl and headed for the door.

"Thank you for your kindness to us. May Allah bless you," she said as she kissed my hand.

We stood at the door, watching our stranger disappear. When we could see her no longer, Ronnalee turned to me and asked, "Was that Baby Jesus?"

"No," I whispered, my thoughts wandering to the Baby of long ago who, like this infant, had been born in a cold mountain village and wrapped in swaddling cloth. "That was just one of the least of His little ones."

CHAPTER 29

COUNTDOWN TIME

January of 1952 arrived and I was looking forward to furlough time in May, 1953—just a year and five months away. Even though we were having a marvelous time in Lebanon, I couldn't wait to see my parents and siblings again. The ideal set-up for me would be to live in Lebanon with my relatives. Lebanon had all kinds of advantages—good people, climate, housing, and medical help. By now they were growing almost every type of food available anywhere. The merchants' shops were filled with goods from all over the world. If any country made it, Lebanon had it. Lebanon was fast becoming a super modern country. No, I didn't want to leave Lebanon or the people permanently, I just wanted to go on furlough.

While I thought furlough, America, home, and loved ones, Wayne thought work—so much yet to do and so little time. By this time Maurice Katrib* had joined us as our translator. In March the men rented a house in Tripoli and began an evangelistic effort. We did very little public advertising because we did not want these meetings to attract a hostile crowd. Since Amuin, we had had almost no opposition. We did put out a few fliers with Wayne and Maurice's pictures on it announcing the time, place, and subject of the meetings. That drew a reasonable crowd, and we were pleased. A few weeks later we passed out a flier with a picture of me playing the accordion, also giving the time, place, and subjects to be presented. That drew an overwhelming crowd. Evidently folks didn't bother to read the leaflet; they just went by the picture and supposed I was giving a concert. Maurice laughed, "Now we know how to pack the house—hand out fliers picturing a lady with an accordion."

The people of the city seemed more interested in being entertained than in Biblical truths. They enjoyed hearing me play the accordion and Maurice sing. They liked getting information and literature that would help them argue with others, but almost no one was converted to Christianity in Tripoli. At the time, we considered the effort a failure because there were few immediate results. It seemed we could never remember that some seeds drop deep into the soil, and it takes a long time for them to surface—sometimes years. (The next year Toufic Issa and family moved to Tripoli and established the work there.)

The gospel message was making real inroads in the towns of El-Koura. Many people with whom we studied during the last year of our work in North Lebanon accepted Jesus teachings and became Adventist Christians then or after we left. Many of them entered church work. In fact, by 1952 some of our early converts had already received their college degrees and were working for the mission.

When school bells rang again for the children of Farhazier, David was four, and Ronnalee was six. I was teaching Ronnie the DICK AND JANE books and her numbers at home, but she wanted to go to a real school. So some days Germana would take Ronnie to visit her Arabic school in the village. Ronnie loved every minute of her visits and talked about it at great length. This made David anxious to attend school too. He wanted a part of what he thought was the good life. About the tenth time he begged Germana to take him too, Ronnie tried to talk him out of it. "David, you have to sit real still and not say one word."

"I can do that," David affirmed.

"No, you can't," Ronnie argued, "You don't even sit through church very good. When Mommy is playing the organ and Daddy is leading out in church, you crawl under the chairs and run away. The last time Nada found you chasing a poisonous snake, you stupid kid."

"It didn't bite me. I'm not stupid. I don't run away from church now," David insisted. This was true. David hadn't escaped from church since he was three, but Ronnie wouldn't let him forget his "unpardonable" toddler behavior.

Sweet little Germana yielded to David's pleas. She got permission from the teacher to take David to school. "Let him try school. If he runs away, it won't matter," Germana laughed.

David held his head high as he trudged off to school with Ronnalee and Germana. He even took a lunch along—food was high on David's list of priorities. Two hours later I heard the front door open and in walked David.

"Why are you home early, David?" I asked.

"I've learned everything already," he answered rather nonchalantly.

"But it takes years of schooling to learn everything," I suggested trying to use logic on my four-year-old.

"No, it doesn't. It's easy. The teacher taught us the alphabet. Alif, bay, tay..." and David completed the alphabet in Arabic.

"That's very good, David. I'm proud of you, but there's still a lot more for you to learn," I reasoned.

"No, there isn't. When we got to zed (Z), I asked the teacher what came next, and she said, 'Nothing comes after zed. That's all.' So I learned it all and I came home. I didn't like school much anyway."

I laughed at his innocence, but I thought how much his attitude typified adults who are satisfied that their knowledge is complete when they have learned only the basics. How many adults had we met during the past five years who thought they knew everything about being Christians simply because they could make the sign of the cross and attended church on Sundays. Few people enjoy the more abundant life in Christ because, like David, they stop with "Z" and think they've learned it all. Many Christians in this world never get beyond this elementary phase in their spiritual life and miss the joy of a deeper, fuller, personal relationship with Jesus.

The days of 1952 slipped quickly into eternity. Teaching the Scriptures, baptizing converts, treating the first aid patients, entertaining guests, and caring for our family made up our daily routine.

January of 1953, the year of our furlough, arrived and I was back on my feet. I was especially thankful to be on the mend knowing that others in my condition had already died of colitis. Once again I was able to eat most foods and be physically active like the rest of the world.

My birthday was January 14, and, since I was well enough to enjoy life again, we decided to celebrate by going up to the Cedars of Lebanon. Wayne and I had both been raised in states that had winter snows, so every once in awhile we satisfied that nostalgia by driving to the higher elevations where we could enjoy the "cold stuff". We never got snow in our area; therefore, a picnic in the snow was a special treat for our children as well.

COUNTDOWN TIME

We packed the car with warm clothing, sandwiches, and hot chocolate and headed for the Cedars.

We spent the day sliding down the slopes in my metal dish pan or on slabs of cardboard. Just before sundown we started home. On the way, I developed a headache so severe that it frightened us. I never got headaches, so how I developed such a walloping head pain was a mystery to us.

We arrived back in El-Koura on time for the scheduled meeting in Bishmizeen. But by now Wayne was afraid to leave me alone with the children. He asked one of the capable members in Bishmizeen to conduct the service that evening. Then we drove the two miles home to Farhazier. Wayne helped me into the house, fed the children, and tucked them into bed. Wayne gave me hot and cold water treatments, aspirin, etc., but I kept nothing down and nothing made me feel better.

Suddenly, miraculously, about 8:30 my headache left me completely. Within seconds the pain was gone. I felt refreshed, which was even more mystifying.

"Well, I'm glad that's over," Wayne remarked, "but you should have gotten well an hour and a half ago so I could have been at the meeting. You timed that just right. Now the meeting in Bishmizeen is over. Are you sure you didn't plan this headache so I would stay home with you on your birthday?" he teased.

"You'd better believe I did. You know I'm a scheming woman," I replied. We laughed and went into the kitchen for a snack.

About 9:30 p.m. we started to study our Sabbath School lesson when we heard screams in the distance. My heart palpitated in fear as the eerie sound came closer to the center of the village and our house.

"It's terrifying," Wayne whispered hoarsely. "Something horrible must have happened."

Then someone stumbled up our front steps and knocked at the door. "Help me. Please someone help me," the person cried.

"Don't open the door!" I warned Wayne. "He may be a drunk, or a maniac, or worse."

Then the person shrieked, kicked, and clawed at our front door.

"I have to open it," Wayne said as he turned the key in the lock. "Someone is in distress!"

"So am I," I said as I headed for safer territory away from the door.

Wayne opened the door cautiously; a man, torn and bloody, fell inside. Wayne helped him into a chair. The man wept uncontrollably and motioned for Wayne to close and lock the door. Wayne obliged, and the man seemed somewhat relieved. After awhile he gained his composure and told his story.

He had been driving on the road between Bishmizeen and Farhazier shortly after 8:30—or the same time Wayne should have been coming home on the same road. As he rounded the halfway bend, suddenly a blaze of fire was lit on the road directly in front of him. He screeched to a halt. He could not drive around the fire because at that spot in the road there is a high stone wall on either side. Before he could turn around, men jumped out from behind the walls and surrounded his car. "Get out with your hands up," they shouted. Then the highway robbers took all of his money and valuables, roughed him up, threw him against the wall, and disappeared among the olive trees. Dazed and frightened the victim ran to Farhazier. He called in the streets for help but no one answered his pleas. When he saw our light was still on, he hurried to our door. We hadn't been willing "good Samaritans" but found ourselves helping the robbed man, anyway. We dressed his wounds, gave him some hot tea, and took him back to get his car. The fire was out and the men were gone. The grateful man drove on to his destination and Wayne came home.

"I know now why you had that headache," Wayne said as he picked up his Bible and Sabbath School quarterly again. "God didn't want me to become a victim of the highway robbers."

"How true!" I agreed. "I wonder how many times God has spared our lives during the past six years. I guess we'll never know until we reach heaven. We've surely been in some tight spots."

"We surely have," Wayne commented, heaving a sigh. "We never lacked for excitement."

"I would have been happy to do without most of the excitement," I said remembering the nights we were stoned or threatened in other ways. "But now that it's countdown time, I'm glad we stayed in North Lebanon and pioneered the work."

"All the credit goes to God, not us. He directed us every step of the way. I shall never cease to marvel at His personal interest in opening the work here in North Lebanon. I would never have known such an intimate relationship with God had it not been for what we've been through. God made me feel like His associate as He spoke to us through opened doors or strong impressions. These years will forever remind me of how closely heaven is "in touch with earth."

"Amen!" I answered fervently as we dropped to our knees for prayer.

MIDGE IN LEBANON

* Maurice Katrib became the editor of Middle East Press in 1954 and served in that capacity until 1977. Part of that time he also was Publishing Secretary for Middle East Division, with the exception of the two years he spent in Evangelism.

Going on a furlough. In Europe, we had too much luggage!

CHAPTER 30

FINAL DAYS

Spring is the time of beginnings, and March 18, 1953 was a special beginning for us. On that day, Elders Appel and Hartwell, George Yared, and Arthur Fund came to North Lebanon to look over the land we had selected for a church and school in Bishmizeen. They voted unanimously to buy the property as soon as possible so that these buildings could be completed by autumn. We worked hard to finalize the purchase of the land and get building permits during the next few weeks. It had been our fondest dream to sign papers that would permanently establish a headquarters for our work in El-Koura. But things did not move as quickly as we had hoped, so that privilege was left to Dan and Gladys Kubrock, our successors.

We planned another baptism for May 16, just before we would leave on furlough. One night we visited Venice Simaan who had been enthusiastically preparing for baptism. We were very surprised, therefore, by her reluctance to consent to the rite. Finally tears welled up in her eyes, and she revealed her problem. "In my old church we pay the clergy for baptizing us as babies. I want to pay Pastor Olson whatever he charges for his services, but I don't have the money right now. I wanted to pay God the back tithe I didn't know I should have paid earlier, so last Sabbath I gave Him all the money I had saved. Now I don't have the money to be baptized. I need to earn some more money."

I took her trembling hands in mine. "Venice, my dear, salvation is free. It is the gift of God. There is no charge in our church for baptizing someone—EVER. We wouldn't think of it."

"Really?" she questioned, her eyes wide with surprise and relief. "Really?"

I nodded my head and smiled. "Really, Venice. Baptism costs you nothing."

She jumped to her feet and twirled about. "Praise God! Oh, thank you for making that clear, Mrs. Olson. I want to be baptized. Count me as one of the candidates on Sabbath."

So Venice joined Mona Razzouk, Henry, Elias, Esperansa, and Mary Jeha down at Jonah's Bay for the baptismal service. It was a wonderful, yet sad occasion for us. It was the last baptismal service we conducted in North Lebanon.

The final days were upon us. We finished our packing and sold or gave away our possessions. The children had been so anxious to go to America, but now that the time had come, they weren't so sure. They would miss their Lebanese friends just as we would. They wanted to leave a token of love with their best friends. David gave one of his favorite cars to Ramon Jeha, the little boy who lived downstairs (and to whom Wayne had given penicillin injections the first week we arrived in Farhazier). Ronnalee debated about her gift to Germana, but at last she decided to give up her best and most loved dolly to her friend. I was touched by my children's sacrificial spirit and love for their friends.

It was with difficulty that we put our bags into our car on Sunday morning to go to Beirut. Hundreds of people crowded the street in front of our house, wishing us Godspeed. We all wept together as we bid one another

FINAL DAYS

farewell. I probably hugged and kissed some people twice as I made the rounds, but I didn't care. El-Koura had been my home for almost five years, and it held precious memories that would last me a lifetime. The Lebanese people, with few exceptions, had been very good to us. Amuin too, one might ask? YES. Amuin too. The people of Amuin were wonderful. They couldn't help that a few of their people chose to cause us trouble. But all of that was now in the past. Peace for Adventists in North Lebanon had been established forever.

Wayne stood on the veranda and asked the people to bow their heads with us as he asked God's blessing to rest upon all the people of El-Koura and us now that we were separating. There was a volume of "amens", more tears and "God be with yous".

Then we climbed into our missionary car and pulled away from the house that had been home and the village folks who had been family to us for five years. I cried half the way to Beirut. I wasn't as thrilled about furlough time as I had thought I would be. Parting with the best friends in the world was traumatic.

I thought back over the six and a half years we had spent in Lebanon. They had been the best of times and the worst of times in my fife. I remembered how God guided us providentially through perilous situations and opened doors before us, His miracles of protection and healing, the joy of bringing the message of salvation to hundreds of people, the blessed privilege of living with the Lebanese, and hundreds of other things for which I could praise God. Was I glad I left America for Lebanon? Absolutely. I had no regrets.

On May 21 we boarded our ship, the M.S. Enotria, for Italy. Many of the missionaries, our Adventist people, as well as a bus load of friends from North Lebanon, were on the dock to wave farewell.

MIDGE IN LEBANON

As our ship pulled out into the Mediterranean Sea and headed West we watched our friends on the dock recede into the distance. The last thing we could distinguish was Anees, Haddad waving Shahin's red sweater.

"Goodbye, fair Lebanon," I murmured through my tears. "We'll see you again in a year. God will bring us back." And He did.

APPENDIX

ABOU JAOUDE FAMILY

Adul	teacher
Faiza	teacher, still serving faithfully in Lebanon.
Habeeb	book store manager
Najla	worked in Voice of Prophecy office.
Nassima	teacher.
Salaam	minister in Cyprus, Lebanon, Jordon, Iraq. Middle East Union departmental leader. Minister in Washington Conference.

AKAR FAMILY

Alfred	teacher, principal, computer analyst.
Jehad	nurse. Taught nursing at Andrews University and Lebanon.
Laurice	teacher. Married Farris Bishi. Missionary to Sudan.
Najah	teacher, Lebanon.
Nabeh	business
Widad	Bible worker. Married pastor George Issa.
Adul, Abdullah, Nour	—professionals, gainfully employed in various places.

DEEB FAMILY

Lorna — married George Yared, treasurer of Lebanon-Syria.

Mary — teacher/secretary. Married Moses Ghazal.

Viola — she, her husband, and six children were shot in their home during the uprisings in Lebanon.

Alma, Leila, and Rita—professionals, married.

HADDAD FAMILY

Anees — Lebanon-Syria youth leader, Middle East Division youth and temperance director. Dr. Haddad served as chairman of the Department of Sociology, Loma Linda, and as Dean of the College of Arts and Sciences.

Edmond — mechanical engineer. Head of Math/Science Department Middle East College. Dr. Haddad was President of Middle East College.

Mary — registrar, Middle East College. Assistant registrar and associate professor, La Sierra College. Married Ignatius Yacoub.

JABBOUR FAMILY

Antoine — teacher, Middle East College, La Sierra College.

JEHA FAMILY

Afeef — teacher, Adventist Schools in Lebanon.

APPENDIX

Elias	teacher, Principal of Adventist Schools in Lebanon (30 yrs).
Esperansa	Secretary, Middle East Press.
Henry	teacher, Principal of Adventist schools in Lebanon.
Mary	teacher, Adventist Schools in Lebanon.
Michael	business, Lebanon.

MELKI FAMILY

Henry	colporteur leader, Middle East Union. Arabic teacher, business manager, Middle East College.
Edmund	moved to Australia where he colporteured for a time.
Hyatt	married, lives in U.S.

MUELLIM FAMILY

Alice	seamstress, cared for her parents until their death.
Elias	works at U.S. Embassy, Beirut (35 years).
Nada	Bible worker in Lebanon. Married American Marine John Hancock who works at Pacific Press.

Khalil and Nadeem—immigrated to America, successful businessmen.

NABTI FAMILY

Michael	dean/teacher, Middle East College. Representative of the League of Arab States in the U.S.; Middle East area

	curator at the Hoover Institution on war, revolution and peace, and frequent panelist on **PBS**. Dr. Michael and his wife, Dr. Patricia, are on the Stanford University staff.
Najwa	librarian, Middle East College and the University of Southern California dental school. Currently librarian at USC's Science and Engineering department.
Salwa	teacher.

Nabeh and Fareed—both have their Ph.D.'s.

NASSIMIAN, MARY—teacher, nurse. Married Ramon Bitar, a worker at the Middle East Press

RAZZOUK FAMILY

Akram II	doctor, M.D. (graduate of Loma Linda University), psychiatrist, Hindsdale Adventist Hospital (Illinois).
Anees	doctor, M.D. (graduate of Loma Linda University), neo-natal heart specialist, works with world-famous Dr. Bailey.
Nabil	Ph.D in business. Teacher, Andrews University, La Sierra College, and California State College.
Naji	M.B.A. business. Worked at Middle East College and La Sierra College.
Najwa	a Christian mother.

APPENDIX

SHAHIN FAMILY

George	teacher, technician.
Samir	minister, Middle East Union, and mission president.

SHAMMAS FAMILY

Edmond	petroleum engineer, a leader in his field.

Adell, Emil, Laurice, Yvette—All special friends who remained in Lebanon.

SIMAAN FAMILY

Abu Jabbour	the father, raised his five children alone after his wife's death. Most became Adventists. Jabbour - physio-therapist (graduate of Loma Linda University).
Odette	nurse, Ben Ghazi Adventist Hospital, Libya. Married Dr. Johnson.
Venice	Bible worker. Married Pastor George Khoury.

Saada and Yvonne—still in Lebanon. Some of their children became Adventists. Saada has three doctor sons, and Yvonne, one.

* There are others from the above listed families who became professionals. With few exceptions, I have tried to limit the appendix to those who became denominational workers at one time or another. Some names I listed are just special people in the same family.

** Most Arabs take pride in work. They are keen business people and capable professionals. It is practically impossible to find a welfare recipient among them.

MIDGE IN LEBANON

We lived among the Arabs for 17 years and found them to be clean, kind, ambitious, and hospitable. Although it is true that lack of water or economic reverses have forced some Arabs to live below comfortable living standards, I hope my fellow Americans will avoid making degrading generalizations about a people who are as diverse and interesting as anyone in the world. I trust that Americans will learn to appreciate and understand these nations of wonderful people as we have. If I could chose my neighbors, it would be Lebanese.

*** We praise God for the protection He gave us in North Lebanon and for the people who became our sisters and brothers in Christ. We hope to spend an eternity with them in the new earth where violence and opposition will be no more.

TEACH Services, Inc.
P U B L I S H I N G

We invite you to view the complete
selection of titles we publish at:
www.TEACHServices.com

We encourage you to write us
with your thoughts about this,
or any other book we publish at:
info@TEACHServices.com

TEACH Services' titles may be purchased in
bulk quantities for educational, fund-raising,
business, or promotional use.
bulksales@TEACHServices.com

Finally, if you are interested in seeing
your own book in print, please contact us at:
publishing@TEACHServices.com

We are happy to review your manuscript at no charge.

www.ingramcontent.com/pod-product-compliance
Lightning Source LLC
Chambersburg PA
CBHW050650170426
43200CB00008B/1225